A Grand and Fabulous Notion

National Parks Centennial

1885

1985

Centenaire des parcs nationaux

DATE DUE	
JUN 1 3 1986	
JUN 1 3 1986 —	*gift*
SEP 8 1986	
OCT 1 6 1986	
SEP 2 7 1988	
APR 6 1989	
MAR 2 8 1990	
SEP 1 0 1992	
APR 1 1 1995	
NOV 2 4 1996	

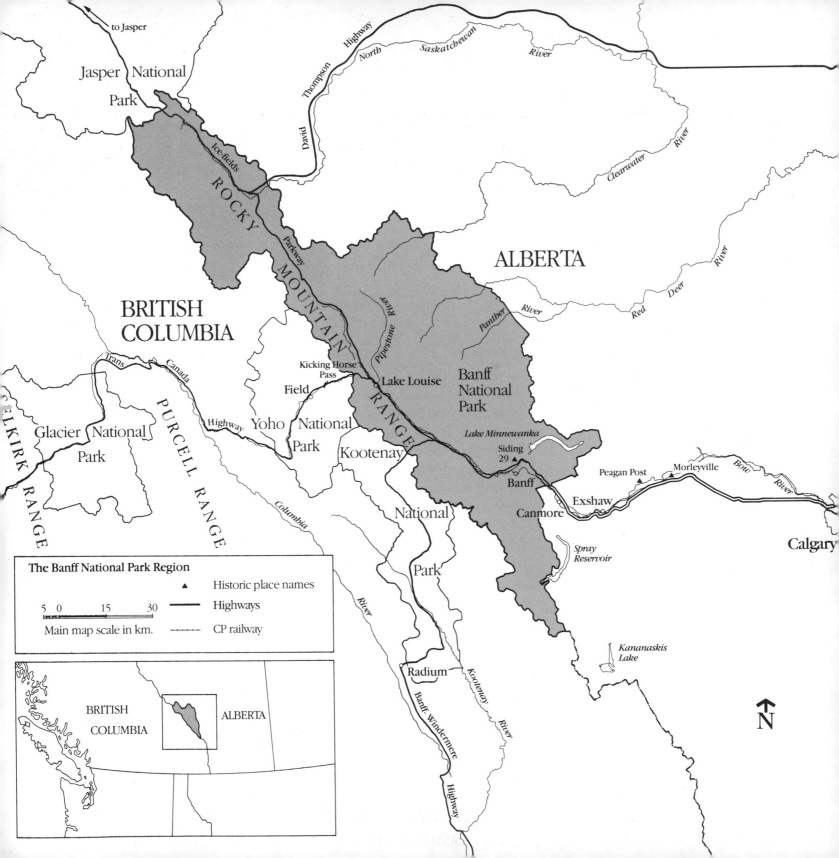

to Jasper

Jasper National Park

ROCKY

Ice-fields

David

Thompson

North

Saskatchewan

River

Clearwater

River

BRITISH COLUMBIA

MOUNTAIN

Parkway

Pipestone River

Panther

River

ALBERTA

Red

Deer

River

Kicking Horse Pass

Lake Louise

Banff National Park

Field

RANGE

SELKIRK RANGE

Glacier National Park

Trans

Canada

PURCELL RANGE

Highway

Yoho National Park

Kootenay

Lake Minnewanka

Siding 29 ▲

Banff

Peagan Post ▲

Morleyville ▲

Bow

River

Calgary

Columbia

National

Canmore

Exshaw

River

Park

Spray Reservoir

Kananaskis Lake

The Banff National Park Region

▲ Historic place names

5 0   15   30

Main map scale in km.

━━━ Highways

┈┈┈ CP railway

Radium

Banff-Windermere

Kootenay

River

River

Highway

BRITISH COLUMBIA

ALBERTA

N

A Grand and Fabulous Notion
The First Century of Canada's Parks

SID MARTY

Preface by Earle Birney

Published by NC Press Limited
in co-operation with Cave and Basin Project,
Parks Canada and the Canadian Government Publishing Centre,
Supply and Services Canada

Jacket photography by:
  Front — Bruno Engler
  Back — Carole Harmon, Brian Patton,
      — Craig Richards, Bruno Engler (hard cover only)
  Flap — R. W. Sandford (hard cover only)
Jacket Design by Fernley/Hesse
Interior Design by Joseph Solway
Typesetting by Perly's Maps Limited, Toronto
Colour Separations by Herzig-Sommerville Limited, Toronto
Printed and Bound by Aprinco Limited, Toronto

Canadian Cataloguing in Publication Data
Marty, Sid, 1944

    A grand and fabulous notion

Bibliography: p.
Includes index.
ISBN 0-920053-07-6 (bound). — ISBN 0-920053-05-X (pbk.).

1. National parks and reserves — Canada — History.
2. Banff National Park (Alta.) — History.
3. National parks and reserves — Canada — Planning.

FC215.M37 1984   333.78'3'0971   C84-099012-X
F1011.M37 1984

We would like to thank the Canada Council and the Ontario Arts Council for
their assistance in the publication of this book.

Published by NC Press Limited
31 Portland Street
Toronto, Ontario, Canada
M5V 2V9

Contents

Index of Colour Plates

Picture Credits

Preface

It's a special pleasure for me to welcome Banff's Centennial and the publication of this book, for I spent the happiest days of my youth in the town and then later as a roaming worker in its national park.

During the summer of 1911, my parents and I lived in a tent on the banks of the Bow and, for most of the next dozen years, in the home my Dad built, which still stands, looking up at Cascade Mountain from Squirrel Street. He would have loved this book too, for he himself was a pioneer and treasured history. He had ridden a horse from Chicago to Calgary before the CPR got there, and went on to travel for years through a good deal of the Pacific Northwest, first as a cowpuncher in the Bow Valley and later as a prospector in the Rockies and the Selkirks.

I'm especially happy to see the emphasis that Sid Marty has placed on the role the thermal springs of Banff played in the development of town and park. Certainly the various springs remain central in my memory. The second morning after my mother and I joined my father, he took us by horse-and-buggy to the Cave and Basin. A boy from the Ponoka bush, it was the first time I'd been in water both warm enough and deep enough to swim in — and I couldn't swim. But there was a blessed rope stretched across the pool, to launch out from and come clinging back to, until I learned the dogpaddle. Later, there were the hundreds of free-for-schoolboy-swims on weekends, diving (illegally, of course) from the Basin's "umbrella" of tufa overhang, and then startling any tourist watcher by seeming not to come up, until I'd wriggled through an underwater "chimney," and burst into air.

The Cave was less fun but more eerie. There was a strange old caretaker, a Mr. Galletley, who always wore a tam o'shanter. He would lead us by lantern through a damp tunnel into a big round cave. The centre was all dark, smelly water, burping up from what Mr. Galletley said were lava beds but he could never explain how the water got there.

He told Scottish jokes to my mother because she was a Scot too. She would try not to laugh at them, but finally she would. They were not nice ones, she said, but I could never understand them or figure out when he was telling what my father called "tall tales." My father said that Mr. G. was right to say the Indians used these springs before the Whites came, but he doubted that the old man had actually seen grizzlies soaking in the Basin to cure their rheumatism.

At ten I became one of the boys with bikes, and took part in expeditions to watch the buffalo in their park, or fish at Minnewanka, or reach a trail up Rundle. But more often, we came to skinny dip in the springs — the Middle ones where adults seldom came. Or the Upper ones, where mushrooms grew enormous under the moss-boxed pipes carrying the thermal water down to the CPR Hotel for the richer tourists, or to Dr. Brett's Sanitarium.

And there was the tepid little pool along the shore of the Third Vermilion Lake where I never went till the winter I was eighteen, swinging a twelve-pound sledge with a rock-drilling crew. We kept our lunch-buckets warm in twenty-below weather by suspending them in the warm hole that the mysterious tufa was maintaining in the lake-ice below the cliffs of the Sawback.

Now I am eighty, and much has changed, with Banff as with me. But the rains fall as before, and sink through crevices high behind Sulphur Mountain to the ancient fires, and come boiling up again for the delight and comfort of Banff boys and tourists and hoteliers and, who knows, perhaps for a gouty old bear or two.

"The Cave is the entrance to the other world."

Earle Birney
April 1984.

Hunger Makes A Hunter

*T*he blue river runs through the famous mountain town. It's late August, and the sun-drenched festival of summer nears its end. Clouds come out of ambush behind Cascade Mountain, brandished like clubs in the fist of the north wind. The wind howls through the feast of flesh parading up Banff Avenue in shorts, T-shirts, and halter tops. This brief display of summer's bounty will soon be over. The rain that freshened the valley last night left a filigree of snow on the summits. A wave of limestone rises above the bustling town, above the surface of the present life. The stone is the stratified bed of a primeval ocean, uplifted by forces in the earth's core that are still not understood. Entire ranges shifted slowly westward over millennia of time. The earth is wrinkled like a gigantic carpet by the ponderous waltz of its continental plates.

Huge glaciers shaped the great domes of limestone, chisels of ice gouged out the hanging valleys, carving out cirques and forming the peaks we see today. The process, repeated many times over the past million years, is in a stage of hiatus in our own brief interval here. The lower Bow Valley has been free of ice for about twelve thousand years: a mere blink of Time's eye. The great ice has retreated to the continental divide for now, where it gnaws slowly on the backbone of North America, biding its time . . . .

We move among familiar pines and smell resin heated by the sun. Beneath our feet, in the ancient bedrock, are the bones and shells of a natural history that began over five hundred million years ago. We have but to strike two pieces of rock together here to smell the elemental odour of the past: sulphur. It's found in the earliest protoplasm, in the cells of the creatures whose limy skeletons now form part of these limestone mountains. In comparison the history of man is but a glimmer of firelight in a vast cave of infinity. Yet the camp fires of hunters and gatherers have sparkled in the mountain nights of Banff National Park for at least ten thousand years.

Working in the Bow Valley, Parks Canada archaeologists have found eighty-four campsites left by an ancient mountain culture whose origins date back to the end of the last glacial epoch. Excavation has barely begun in the other park valleys; the Red Deer, Panther, and Clearwater, north of Banff townsite. Campsites and artifacts, buried hearths, arrowheads, stone tools, and piles of splintered, burnt bones have also been found in the other mountain national parks.

Thousands of years before the advent of the bow, an ancient people hunted bison,

"Thousands of years before the advent of the bow, an ancient people hunted bison."

deer, and mountain sheep in these valleys, armed only with stone-tipped spears, butchering their kill with stone knives. Little is known about their way of life, their ordeals and triumphs, or what gods, if any, they may have set up at the edge of the sentinel glaciers. What is known is that the Kootenay Indians and their relatives, the *Tona xa*, had occupied these mountains and the adjacent ranges in eastern British Columbia for perhaps two thousand years. These Indians retreated west across the mountains following disastrous smallpox epidemics early in the seventeenth century. Who occupied the region before the *Tona xa* may never be known, but I think of their mysterious ancestors as the "Old Ones."

The Old Ones were opportunistic hunters and gatherers who found protection in the mountains from the tearing north wind that scourges prairie dwellers. The warm Chinook often blows in these mountains, bringing mild spells in mid-winter, providing a range for the big game animals. From the native chert (a flint-like stone) of the mountains, they quarried supplies to fashion hide-scrapers, stone hammers, and lance points. One of their quarries was located just a kilometre north of Banff townsite. The Old Ones used *atlatls* (spear throwers) to kill bison, deer, and mountain sheep. Using crude fences of dead timber, they forced the sheep to the edge of a precipice or into some cul-de-sac where they brought their deadly spears into play. Deer trapped by deep snow in their winter yards, bison ambushed while swimming lakes or stampeded into a muskeg, became targets for these mountain hunters.

Like their aboriginal descendants, the Old Ones could not have lived on meat alone. They knew the local food and medicine plants. They cached their crops of wild roots, berries, and herbs in primitive root houses lined with bark to keep out rodents, and covered with pine needles to keep out frost. Fish, scorned by some plains tribes, was relished by the Old Ones. They angled for trout with hooks made of crossed bone splinters. Stone net-sinkers have been found in the mountain parks; the Old Ones netted migrating fish near the mouth of the Waterton River in today's Waterton Lakes National Park. Even in winter, the historic Kootenay were known to set their nets of split spruce roots under the river ice, catching migrating ling.

The Bow Valley has always been a main axis of transmontane travel. The Old Ones, the Kootenay and Stoney Indians, the fur traders, explorers and surveyors — all have left a record in the mountain earth. Their camps are found anywhere where the four prerequisites for man's habitations can be met: water, food, fuel, and a southern exposure to the low winter sun. Unfortunately, many of the old campgrounds have been destroyed by railroad and highway construction since the turn of the century.

Today, the men and women of Parks Canada's Historic and Archaeological Research Section monitor any development in the national and historic parks that might destroy this hidden heritage. One that received their attention was the renovation of the Cave and Basin Hot Springs building on Sulphur Mountain just west of Banff townsite. These thermal springs were formally declared a National Historic Site by Parks Canada in 1982, and the archaeologists were there to supervise some of the excavations, and do some digging of their own.

On this terraced mountain, where the Canadian national parks system was born a century ago, the scientists were confronted with an archaeological nightmare. The earth they explored with their square-edged spades and sharp mason's trowels had been spaded, graded, and excavated countless times in the course of development of the springs. This made it difficult to identify layers in the soil that might indicate the age of any artifacts found. They found plenty of cast-off debris left by white men over the past hundred years. But to an archaeologist, a century is a mere blink of history's hoary eye. As Parks Canada's Don Steer once told me, "To us, a hundred years is sort of embarrassing. Like poking around in Grandma's old trunk without her permission."

At the Cave and Basin, the scientists worked with the smell of history in their nostrils, courtesy of the hot sulphur springs, while the noise of modern machinery assailed their ears. The old bathhouse was being restored by scores of workmen for the centennial of Banff National Park. Ignoring the distractions, the scholarly diggers followed a trail of bone splinters two metres deep into the past and, to their delight, unearthed the skull of a buffalo that showed the yellow varnish of great age. It seems that where there are bison, prehistoric man is never far behind. They kept an eye on a backhoe digging a new drainage line nearby as they explored their test pits.

"Working in the Bow Valley, Parks Canada archaeologists have found eighty-four camp-sites left by an ancient mountain culture."

*   *   *

The machine bites deep into the saturated ground, into the tufa, the crumbling mineral deposited by the hot springs over the centuries. The engine growls and the iron bucket lifts, pivots, and opens its jaws. The muck slides out, but something long and yellow glints wetly, caught in the bucket's open maw.

"Hold it!"

The operator keeps the bucket steady, as they hurry over. Rain begins to fall and the shadows of late afternoon lengthen and give way to evening. The lights of town are blurred and drowned in the marsh and river. They shimmer and dance over the mirroring waters. Long ago the present townsite was a lake bed, and it seems as if the water might rise again, in the long sibilance of falling rain, to claim sovereignty. In the morning the mountain tops will surround the town with raised white lances of snow.

*   *   *

"The snow feeds the Great Ice," said the man they called Hawaxso, "the Singer." "Here it has already melted, and our tracks with it. Except under the pines they'll stay a little while."

The boy thought about his tracks staying somewhere when he was elsewhere, but the thought confused him, and he gave it up. Below the Mountain-Where-the-Water-Falls, all trails crossed at a nexus of open meadow, where water and fuel were close at hand. Hungry, and fearful, the tribe had built their *wiki-ups*, shelters of deadfall, covered with bark.

Far to the north, heat waves shimmered on the white dome of an ice sheet that blocked the valley. An ice-fall up that way boomed and echoed among the peaks that ringed their camp. The boy jumped and stared toward the glacier. His father Gtupin, "Young Pine," had gone up there the day before to scout for game. He glanced to where his mother, cheeks sunken with hunger and fatigue, sat by the fire. Ten days before, she had left a still-born infant in a burial pit lined with fir boards that he and his father, Gtupin, had split with an antler wedge and stone hammers. He knew she would not smile again until his father returned.

"I am tired," was all she would say when he spoke to her. But now the other women had seen fish again in the unknown river near the camp, and the girls were digging roots. His stomach rumbled with hunger.

Not far from camp his grandfather, Hawaxso, had found an outcrop of flint where a creek debouched onto the meadow. The old man had brought a chunk of it to work into lance points. He was perched beside his favourite grandson now, talking as the boy worked at the blank of flint with an antler pick. The ice spoke again, like long thunder. "Ha!" cried the old man, gratified. He was always the last to feel hunger in his long, sunken belly. "The ice cries out against the sun, for making it sweat as it wrestles with the rock. But it goes on, grinding down the rock to make the mountain earth, the earth that grows the grass and pines."

The boy missed a stroke with his pick. He bit his lip to avoid crying out. "How can grass grow from stones like this, Grandfather?" he asked, holding up the slab of dark chert.

Lance points.

"Not from stones, but from the stones ground down into white silt. You have seen how a river runs white as it leaves the Great Ice?"

Yes, he had seen it.

"It leaves the silt in banks here and there, as it wanders. And it forgets to go back for it, and flows somewhere else. And the grass grows." As he spoke, he worked with a flint-pointed hand drill to bore a hole through a piece of soap-stone he had been carrying for some time. It would make a counter-weight for his new *atlatl*.

"These mountains hold the bones of the dead," he muttered. Now it was as if he spoke to himself. "High on the ridges where the flat stones have fallen down, there are shells of things that must have lived in water, like the river clams do. But now they are turned to stone . . . . "

The boy felt his hackles rise.

"How can this be?" the old man muttered. "Aiee! Yet I have seen it."

The boy didn't like to hear such talk. The thought of grown men being weak filled him with terror.

Hawaxso glanced at the boy. "The bones of the dead feed the grass that feeds the deer and the buffalo, that feeds us. Out on the plain where the sun comes up, I have seen bones of great beasts frozen in the rocks where the river digs deep. Such animals I have never seen, nor ever wish to."

The boy stared at him, frightened now. "How big, Grandfather?"

"Big."

"Bigger than *Ktauta*?" The word was out before he knew it, the forbidden name of the grizzly bear.

"Hush!" hissed his grandfather, putting a hand to the boy's mouth. They both glanced around them looking for eavesdroppers. "Do you want to make that one angry? Your sisters are out gathering sweet roots."

The boy shivered. "There has been no sign on the back trail for two days," he ventured hopefully.

"Ah. Such a one may be hereabouts and leave no sign . . . . " The boy trembled, despite the warm sun on his neck. For over a year, run-ins with grizzly bears had left the people terrified and demoralized. It had started when strangers came into their *amakes*, their territory on the river. Hawaxso had wanted to drive them off, but Hungry Man, his brother's son, had dallied with one of the strange women, and the old man (he was forty-five) had bowed to his brother's defense of Hungry Man. And what was our reward? he asked himself. The strangers conjured against us and sent a grizzly into camp to steal our meat and rob our root cache.

Hawaxso's thoughts were black and bitter. His son Gtupin had wounded the

"The tribe had built their wiki-ups *of dead-fall, covered with bark."*

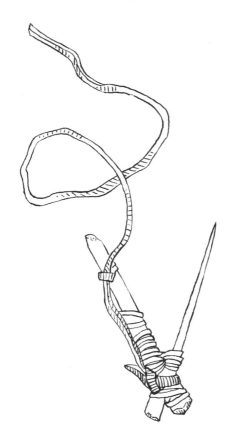

Fishing hooks were made from crossed bone splinters.

Spirit Bear and driven it off, but another came to take its place and wreak more havoc among their bark-covered *wiki-ups*. The winter was lean and miserable. They'd lived on black tree moss, grouse, and rabbits — when they could snare those small fry. Towards the end, until the ling had appeared in the streams, they'd lived on boiled moss, flavoured with grouse droppings. "Memories of grouse" the boy had called it, that bitter soup of famine. "Hunger makes a hunter," he'd replied.

Yes, they had stayed in their lodges like rabbits while up river a conjuror, bound in a bear hide, chanted and worked evil on them. And he, Hawaxso, once a *Yakasin*, hunt leader and great conjuror, had sat as if transfixed, gaping at the fire. In the end, they had left the valley, with a grizzly on their trail for ten days. He had no amulet, no bear claw or cape to ward off the evil.

Hungry Man, never known to feel unwelcome, came over from his *wiki-up* and sat down in the sun below their perch. He broke wind noisily, scratched himself and yawned. The boy bid him good morning. Hawaxso merely grunted. He is a poor man, he told himself, with no spirit guardian. *"K nm na qaqa a ne."* Yes, without a *Nupaka*, he will no doubt die soon.

"My sons have seen the tracks of mountain sheep hereabouts," said Hungry Man importantly.

"Mountain sheep!" cried the boy. "Where?"

Hungry Man didn't answer. "Your father is wasting his time up there. Nothing lives near that ice," he said scornfully.

Hawaxso felt the boy's eyes on him, waiting for his answer. He has questions. Good. Let him learn a little at a time about men, and not forget. He spun the drill between his calloused palms and remained silent.

"Yes, many tracks," said Hungry Man again. He sought constantly to undermine Gtupin's reputation as a hunter. But Hawaxso had already seen the tracks, left by a migrating band of sheep more than five days ago. They had gone up high to the summer range, to escape the flies. It would take ambition to catch up to them, and fuel for the hunter's belly.

"Tracks don't make soup," said Hawaxso quietly.

They were interrupted by a cry from the river. The boy's other uncle with his two wives came up from the stream carrying their nets woven of split spruce roots. The stone netsinkers clinked together as they walked.

"Some char!" cried the youngest, a girl only a year older than the boy. She held the fish up in the sunlight, her fingers hooked under their gill covers, and streams of silver dropped on the rocks. Smelling fish guts, the half-wild dogs of the camp began to whine anxiously and skulked back and forth near the edge of the fire.

The morning fire had died down to a bed of coals. In the pit beneath was a bed of hot rocks that held a layer of avalanche lily bulbs wrapped in black tree moss and willow leaves. A layer of earth separated these from the hot coals on top. Water, funnelled down into the pit a bit at a time, produced the steam to cook the bulbs. Taking a willow branch for a fan, the girl cleared the white ash from the embers, and tossed the fish on the coals where they buckled and stiffened.

"Hu was!" cried the boy, smelling the cooking char.

His aunt laughed. Her girlish voice belied the already womanly set of her eyes. "You are always hungry. And soon you will be hungry for more than bull trout." The boy stared at her, not sure of her meaning. She smiled archly at him and her husband, who had overheard, turned and kicked the nearest dog viciously in the ribs. "Back, thief!" he cried. He glared at the boy, but the look went unnoticed there. Someone had appeared far down the meadow, moving at an easy dog trot: it was his father. Mitsquaquas, the boy's mother, had seen him too, and her look softened. "He has found something," she said. The dogs left off fighting over the fish guts and ran out to meet him. He was the only man they showed any love for. The people were dividing up the fish and roots as he came in, with his spears carried lightly in one hand. Mitsquaquas took food for her family on a square of pine bark and went to her husband. The news would wait until he had eaten.

The people ate in silence, glancing covertly at the hunter, hoping for good luck.

"How is it with you, woman?" he asked warily. Given food and a chance to rest, she was usually as bright and sharp-tongued as the chickadee she was named for.

"Everything passes," she said, knowing it was what he wanted to hear.

He had been secretly relieved at the death of the infant: it was one less belly to fill. But at night he had held her close in a kind of desperation that made her despair: he, too, lived in fear. At length he stood up, wiping his mouth with the back of his hand.

"I have found buffalo," he announced. "A small herd, to the south of us." His voice was drowned in the excitement of the others: "How many? Where did he say?" They had not seen a bison for over a year.

He pointed to the terraced mountain across the valley. "Over the river, below that ridge. There is timber, but not too thick. And there is a swamp in front of them, between them and the river, and more swamp and water on this side of the river."

"Ha! We will drive them into the swamp with the dogs," cried a hunter.

Gtupin nodded. "We must cross the river in two groups, above and below them, and fence them in." The people quieted, thinking of the difficulty.

"We are weak from hard times," said Hawaxso softly, "but buffalo meat will make us fat again!"

"Huh!" interjected Hungry Man. "How did he see these buffalo that hide in the trees across lakes and rivers?"

Gtupin stared at him, his face expressionless, except for the cold glitter in his eyes. *Kpuk!* he thought. All you do is sit on it, and that's all you are. "*Ata!*" he answered sharply, jerking his thumb to indicate the cloud-hung ridge high above their camp that looked out over the valley. "Only climb that mountain," he said coldly, "and you too will see buffalo."

"*Aka!*" cried the boy, stabbing the air with his still unpointed spear. "We will kill many!" The handful of hunters in the little group smiled at his ferocity. He felt the drool form in his mouth at the thought of so much meat, and so much marrow freed from the bones with the blows of a stone hammer.

"Hold still, oh mighty hunter," said his mother who had come up behind him. He felt a sharp tug at the back of his neck. He turned, rubbing the spot, and his mother held up an engorged woodtick, fat as a ripe gooseberry, that had attached itself under his long hair. She tossed it into the fire.

"They bring mountain fever," she told him sternly. "I have told you to look for them after being in the timber. You must check there, too," she added, pointing at his groin, and stepping forward as she did. The boy backed up hurriedly, afraid his mother would lift his bark breechcloth to check for the parasites then and there. He saw his sisters giggling behind their hands, and he gave his mother an angry look.

"Look to your lance, boy," said his father. "You may need it tomorrow."

*   *   *

The bear came into camp so softly, moving against the night wind, that the dogs didn't smell it until it was right among them. Gtupin awoke when he heard the rattle of its claws on the boulders by the stream where the fish had been gutted. Then there was a pandemonium of snarling dogs, a roar, and a splashing noise as the bear took to the river. One dog, nearly decapitated by a blow of an armoured paw, lay twitching on the bank. The whole camp was roused. The people built up their fires again and huddled together, dozing fitfully until dawn. The wolfish dogs sat back from the fire and stared into the night, whining as if with regret, every time a coyote howled.

The hunters set out before first light, leaving a few boys and one old man to help the women strike camp. It was a long and tiring stalk, but not without

rewards. Hundreds of ducks lived among the reeds near the sand dunes that formed the end of the lake. There were pines scattered through the sand.

"Ha! Here are poles to frame a net!" cried Hawaxso, gesturing at the trees. "I
never saw a better place to take ducks."

"Ducks!" scoffed Hungry Man. "They are for women. A hunter eats buffalo!" The old man only smiled his thin smile.

They trotted through the sand; ten hunters and six dogs. The wolf-dogs looked
almost comical in their rawhide muzzles as they strained at their noose-like collars
and rawhide leashes. The boy brought up the rear, as his father had ordered.

Gtupin had stopped and, leaning on his spear, stared at the ground. His face
was strained and tense. Following his look, they saw the print of a grizzly bear
in the sand. "Today may be the day," said Gtupin grimly.

"Do not say it," said Hawaxso anxiously. "We have no power . . . ."

"If our Brother-Across-The-River comes between us and the buffalo," said Gtupin,
"we will have to play with him. You know it." Hawaxso turned pale. He swallow-
ed and nodded his agreement. Hungry Man, for once, was silent. But his scornful
smirk was almost audible.

They waded through the shallows of the river and, climbing the opposite bank,
set off in single file through the timber, always moving at a trot. Each man carried
a spear thrower and several extra spears, tied together with a thong to make them
manageable. In every wet place the bear's tracks were clear for all to see. After
twenty minutes of nervous weaving through a tangle of trees and willow, Gtupin
stopped again, this time turning his head, reading the air currents.

"That smell . . . ."

"Yes," said Hawaxso. "As I thought. There is a lick here of stinking mud. We
must be close . . . ."

The buffalo, in fact, were bedded down within a stone's throw of the
hunters. Wolves had driven the bison across the river from the open slopes they
preferred on the north side of the valley. Drawn by the smell of minerals, the
herd had come down the mountain to the edge of the swamp to lick the dirt between the pine roots. Deer flies swarmed around their shaggy heads and bit them
under the tail and around their small, brown eyes. They would not stay long, but
the heat had made them listless that day. The old bulls gored up the soft earth
with their horns. The herd wallowed in the muck, then bedded down in the shade
to chew their cud, armoured against the flies with hardened mud. The heat made
them lethargic and careless.

Gtupin waved with his arm, and the hunters began to spread out. The deer
flies descended on them, and their bare backs were flecked with blood as they brushed

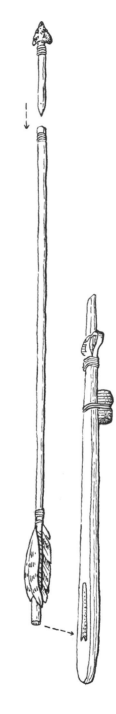
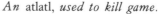

An atlatl, *used to kill game.*

them off. All was silent. Before them was a clearing. Then there came a loon's cry. Gtupin answered it. He motioned his son towards him. "Stay by me," he said softly, "but keep behind. When I tell you, use your lance."

The party waited while Hawaxso and another man climbed up the mountainside, trying to get above the buffalo. In a few minutes, there came the second cry of a loon. The two stole out into the top of the clearing and began to move down the slope. A figure emerged from the opposite side of the woods and joined them: Hungry Man's father, Kimbusco, "Mountain Goat."

Down the mountainside, Gtupin waited impatiently for Hawaxso and the others to come into sight. Hidden in the woods, they heard the soft bleat of a buffalo calf. The animal came out of a willow thicket and looked around, searching for its dam, then disappeared again.

"We must move before the wind shifts," Gtupin whispered. He gave the loon's cry a third time and, slipping the muzzle off his dog, turned it loose. It rushed in the direction of the bleating calf, soon followed by the rest of the pack.

When the savage dogs came out of the woods on either side of the clearing, the buffalo rose in a panic-stricken mass and ran, eyes rolling, down into the swamp. The dogs cut off the last calf to move, fell on it and tore it to pieces before the hunters, running hard to keep up, entered the clearing. They did not stop to drive off the dogs: it would have been dangerous, and a waste of time. They formed a widening semi-circle and splashed into the muskeg after the foundering beasts.

The buffalo bellowed and fought to get to the river where they could swim to freedom. Jumping from hummock to hummock, the hunters speared the thrashing animals that were mired. The boy slipped and fell into the water, as one of the last cows turned in a frantic effort to escape. He caught a glimpse of his father poised above him, his arm going back, fingers outstretched. "Get back!" his father yelled.

He turned to find the cow nearly on top of him, and quickly raised his lance up to her throat. A spear suddenly appeared above her front leg; his lance bent and snapped, then he went under.

Something pulled hard on his head; Gtupin had caught him by the hair. He choked and fought for breath, and saw the sky again. He lay on the bank, winded but unhurt. All the hunters were yelling and singing victory songs. Hungry Man's was the loudest of all, and his feet were the driest. The pools of swamp water were stained a rusty red. Most of the herd had escaped, but four cows and a calf lay in the water. A fifth, with the boy's lance point buried in its lungs, was kicking its last on the bank.

The famished hunters came up and squatted nearby. In the cow's body cavity, Hungry Man made blood soup with tidbits from the organs and some contents of the animal's paunch. The hunters dipped slices of liver in this mess, and ate with blood running down their chins. Their hunger was frightening to watch: the boy turned away.

"Try it!" they urged him. But his stomach churned from the blow the cow had given him.

Gtupin looked around. "Where's my father?" he asked. The hunters shrugged: no one knew. He was about to send the boy after him when the old man appeared. "Have you no shame?" he cried. Gtupin looked up, startled, and wiped his mouth.

"Father! We have killed buffalo!"

The old man nodded. "For which we must be grateful. But why do you not give thanks?" The men looked at each other shamefacedly, except for Hungry Man who went on guzzling.

Gtupin stood up, brandishing his spear with a bloody hand. "Hear me Oh-Chief-Who-Made-Himself, hear me mighty *Iva-Kasin, Ki-nmi-ki!*" he cried. "Your children who were starving, now have meat! The skull of this buffalo we will leave to honour the buffalo Nupaka!"

"Huh. But we'll bash the brains out first!" muttered Hungry Man. His father, Kimbusco, glared at him. "Silence, fool!" he roared, "or we'll leave your head to appease the buffalo Nupaka!"

"For the gift of their flesh, we are grateful," said Gtupin.

"Aiee! We are grateful!" the other hunters chorused fervently.

"Hear me now!" cried Hawaxso. This place is a power place: much medicine I have found up yonder. We have been led here by a mighty hunter, who hunts alone. His teeth are his weapons; his claws are his weapons! His name is Holy! I pledge an offering to him. A buffalo tongue will I give him!"

The hunters leaned on their spears and wondered at his words. Could it be the bear that had haunted their camps was now to be rewarded? Hawaxso pried open the buffalo's jaw, and with his sharp stone knife, cut out its tongue. His eye fell on the broken shaft of the lance buried in the cow's chest.

"It is your grandson's," said Gtupin proudly.

"Ah. This boy has earned a name today: Broken Lance!"

"Ahhh," chorused the hunters approvingly. The boy stood up, pleased but still shaken. He was not used to such attention from the men.

"Cut me a willow for a skewer, Broken Lance, and I will take this offering up the mountain. What I have to show you all must wait; we have much work to do."

About noon the women came in, heavily loaded with the camp goods, the robes, stone tools, and woven rush mats for the lodges. Fires were lit on the river bank and the smell of roasting meat brought smiles and laughter back to the people. The water in the cooking baskets, heated to boiling with hot rocks, gave off a sweet smell of meat, stewed with cattail tubers, wild onions, and mountain sorrel.

Hawaxso supervised the building of a drying rack. The children went to gather willow boughs to smoke the meat, and in the evening, a breeze came off the river and quelled the hordes of flies and mosquitoes that plagued the camp. Hawaxso's clan sat near him, wondering what secret the old man would offer them in the morning. Despite the grizzly bear sign in the forest, the whole camp slept deeply that night and into the full sun of the next day.

"Now," said the old man, when they had filled their bellies once again, "a few must stay and keep the dogs away from our meat. The rest will come with me."

The people filed up the mountain, following the old man. Soon they could smell again the strong stink of sulphur. The mountain steepened, and they came to a stream.

"Huh! The water stinks," said the boy, Broken Lance. He stepped in it, but quickly jumped back in fear, colliding with his mother. "It's warm!" he cried fearfully.

The others felt it, and recoiled, muttering.

"Come!" cried the old man sternly. His voice echoed, as if from a cavity, above them. They climbed up and found him standing by a pool, near the base of a cliff. "Feel it," he commanded them, when they had all assembled.

Timidly, the people slipped their bare feet into the water. "*O ya!*" they cried; it was very warm and their faces perspired as in a sweat lodge when they leaned over the pool.

"Listen to me," said the old man. "We have been led to this place. Up there," he gestured, "there is a cave. I found it yesterday. It is powerful!"

"Ahhh!" cried the people fearfully.

"Listen to me. Last night I dreamed, and in my dream, a Spirit Bear came up out of the cave and spoke to me."

"Ahhh!"

"The cave is the entrance to the other world. It is a forbidden place. None but a Yakasin can go there and live!" he warned. "This is what the Nupaka said to me. 'I have brought you here and given you these buffalo. It was I that drove you from the river. By the cave, you have left an offering: it is good. When you hunt here, you must always do homage, or my curse will be upon you, and you and yours will surely perish. No buffalo, no deer or sheep, will fall to your spears. The pool is my gift to you: it is powerful! It will purify you, and heal your wounds.' These were the words of the Spirit Bear.''

''Now listen to me. Tonight the hunters will bathe in this pool, and then the women. We will feast, and pay homage to the Nupaka, so that the hunting will always be good here, in the Valley-of-the Cave.''

Hungry Man stayed in camp to guard the meat: he didn't mind. It gave him a chance to thieve a bit for his private cache. The other men sat by the fire, having bathed for the first time in hot water. They were awed by the experience. Broken Lance had been allowed to bathe and eat with the men. He was the envy of the other boys.

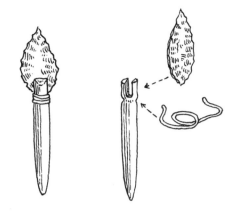

''Gtupin sawed the meat from a buffalo bone with his flint knife.''

They felt soothed, relaxed, and struggled to express themselves. ''Aiee! What heat!'' said one. ''Like lying between two women.'' The men laughed, and from the pool came the answering laughter of the women, echoing from the rocks, over the swamp. Gtupin sawed the meat from a buffalo bone with his flint knife, and offered some to his father and to his son. ''Listen to the women laughing there,'' he said. ''They have not laughed like that for over a year.'' ''We have not eaten like this for over a year,'' said Hawaxso. The red light of the fire played on their lean, weathered faces. Reflected on the cliff above the pool, it shone out over the swamp, dancing on the water, echoed by Hungry Man's fire in the trees below the pool.

''When they laugh like that,'' said Gtupin, ''a man feels life is good.'' The bone was picked clean, and he tossed it across the fire into the trees. It shone for a split second in the ruddy light, then fell through the branches to the forest floor. Dead pine needles pattered down after it. The faces faded as the fire died.

* * *

Pine needles, spruce needles and layers of dust formed over the bone. Lightning, or men, set the forest ablaze; the spruce died, but the ancient pine cones germinated in the heat, and the pines grew again. Until one day, perhaps eight thousand years later, a machine reached down through time and caught the bone, yellowed with age, in its arbitrary steel jaw.

Two men saw the bone shining again in the mountain light. They stood for a moment staring at this cast-off message that a human hand had incised with the marks of a stone knife; a hand bloody with the brutality of survival.

Cautiously, tentatively, as if it were as fragile as the Dead Sea Scrolls, a man's hand reaches down through the ages, the fingers slowly opening to touch the ghostly hands of the past. To acknowledge a voice and another mind that says, ''I too was here by these mysterious springs; I too lived, wondered, and passed by.''

*I*n a wilderness without beginning or end, memory was the only map. Feuds over hunting and fishing grounds were settled on the spot, hand to hand. Plans of conquest centred on the defeat of every winter, upon survival. Horseless and wheel-less, the tribes described their slow orbits through the earth's four seasons, following the caribou and the buffalo.

In the vast quiet of the Stone Age, the voice of nature echoed in men's ears. Trees could still speak then, bringing messages from the dead. Rare stones were found, magically shaped like buffalo by unknown hands. They cried out to be picked up, promising luck in hunting. A spirit dwelt in every corner of creation, and imposed its arbitrary moralities on men, punishing those who denied its edicts.

As a stone breaks the surface of a pool with ever widening ripples, so the arrival of Europeans in the New World sent ripples of change across the land that would someday be called Canada. Word spread through the western tribes of strange beings in the East whose skin was pale as that of a corpse, and whose faces were covered with hair like the moss of trees. Long before the Plains Indians set eyes on these ghostly creatures, they felt the effect of their presence in the land.

With the coming of the Whites, *The People* discovered that power dwelt in the small black mouth of a musket barrel. It could be had by anyone who could match the length of a musket with a pile of beaver pelts.

The Cree, and their allies the Assiniboine, were the first to acquire the new weapons from the traders on Hudson Bay. They began to move ever westward, searching for more beaver, and for buffalo to make pemmican, the staple food of the fur trade. The tribes were pushed against each other as their hunting grounds were gradually overrun.

The Blackfoot of the plains were driven west and south before the invincible warriors, until they clashed with the Crows and the Shoshoni. The Assiniboine, now known as the Stoneys (they used hot stones to boil their meat), were deflected by Blackfoot resistance into the foothills and mountains of the old Kootenay territory. As the Blackfoot fell back to the south, they were assailed, in 1730, by the Shoshoni Indians, mounted on beasts the Blackfoot had never seen before. They named them *"ponokaumita"* meaning "elk dog." This was the tough little cayuse, descended from the proud stock of the Conquistadores, the horse that opened up the West.

Repulsed by their Shoshoni enemies, the Blackfoot fought back, trading for "fire

"And what do they do with all these beaver pelts?"

"Have you not heard? They use them to make hats."

"Aiee! These white ghosts must live in a land of ice!"

sticks'' with their friends the Cree. They captured a few cayuses and eventually raided the tribes as far south as New Mexico to steal more of the priceless beasts. When the first Whites arrived in what is now Alberta, they found that most of the country south of the North Saskatchewan River was ruled by Blackfoot war parties. This savage cavalry, ubiquitous as the prairie wind, controlled the approaches to the mountain passes of southern Alberta until the middle of the Nineteenth Century.

Having once suffered bitterly for lack of horses and guns, the Blackfoot were determined to maintain their superiority. They tried to disrupt trade between the white man and the mountain tribes, the Stoneys and Kootenay. The Stoneys, also known as ''*Wapamathe*,'' the ''Throat Cutters,'' were originally part of the Sioux nation. They soon made themselves masters of the mountains and foothills, but ventured out onto the plains whenever possible to hunt buffalo and steal horses from the Blackfoot. When pressed and outnumbered, they vanished through the great portals of the Rockies, which the Blackfoot seldom entered.

Their trails wound up either side of the Bow River and they roamed north to the Kootenay Plains, and south to Chief Mountain, Montana. Not surprisingly, the hot springs on Sulphur Mountain were a favourite stopping place for these people. Their medicine men regarded the springs as a sacred place to be used after purification by prayer. The area of present-day Banff was a spiritual locus of the tribe. They set up their Sun Dance Lodge and made sacrifices to the sun on the meadows below Bow Falls.

The Stoneys' western neighbours, the Kootenay, worked their way back across their old territory twice a year to hunt buffalo on the plains. They came with their bows in hand, but they also came to trade with bales of beaver pelts and rawhide bags full of ochre from the Vermilion River. This mineral was coveted by the Stoneys and Blackfoot to make face paint. In time, the ancient springs became a peace ground where the two tribes rendezvoused to trade and gamble for horses, blankets, and anything else of value.

To the white traders, like David Thompson of the North West Company, the Bow Valley was *terra incognita.* The traders were confined to the northern passes, the Athabasca and Howse, by the hostile Blackfoot. Thompson penetrated no more than a few kilometres up the Bow in 1801, before the Blackfoot sent him hightailing back north to Rocky Mountain House. In 1832, the Hudson's Bay Company traders bluffed and bribed their way south, to set up Peagan Post near Bow Valley Gap. The Peagans (part of the Blackfoot nation) simply boycotted the post until the Whites abandoned the venture two years later. Then the Indians burned it to the ground.

Right: Horse Race at Morley, Alberta.

Below: Stoney Indian camp on the North Saskatchewan River.

Until the arrival of the railroad surveyors in the 1880s, only nine parties of white travellers are known to have come anywhere near the Banff vicinity. Most of them, like Sir George Simpson, "the Demon Traveller" of the fur trade, were only passersby. But one man, a missionary, made a lasting impression on the *Wapamathe.*

Above the town of Banff rises Mount Rundle, one of the world's most photographed mountains. This great wedge of limestone was named after Robert Terrill Rundle, whose mission to the Stoneys in the 1840s was sponsored by the Hudson's Bay Company. Rundle was a frail Englishman with a big heart, whose Christian generosity earned the respect of the impoverished Stoneys. They listened to his tale of a man who died on two crossed sticks in a fabulous land, for the sake of sinners everywhere. Being natural-born singers, the Indians learned the Christian hymns the good man taught them. They shared their food and lodging with him — they shared everything except their knowledge of the sacred hot springs, part of their old faith, which lay only a few kilometres from the missionary's camp.

After several trips to visit his flock, Reverend Rundle returned to England in 1848 to recoup his health. He left the Stoneys to practice their hymns undisturbed by white visitors for seven years. He had made many converts to Christianity. More importantly, he'd made, by example, many friends for the white men who would follow his trail in the future.

In 1857, the threat of American expansion, coupled with the end of the Hudson's Bay monopoly on trade in the northwest, pushed more outriders of change into Blackfoot country, and up the blue Bow River of the Stoneys.

The British parliamentarians felt the entire area of Rupert's Land should be ruled by the colonial government in Canada. But vast expanses of "The Great Lone Land" were unknown to Europeans. Could farms be established on the plains? How numerous were the inhabitants? What minerals could be mined there? Was there a route across the Rockies for a road to the colony in British Columbia? To answer these questions, an expedition headed by Captain John Palliser headed west in 1857.

In 1858, the Blackfoot were preoccupied by their interminable feud with the Crees. Dr. James Hector, a Scots physician and geologist on the expedition, was able to make his way across the central plains to the site of Old Bow Fort (formerly Peagan Post) unmolested. With three Red River men, Eugene Bourgeau, the expedition's botanist, and "Nimrod," a Stoney guide, Hector rode into the Bow Valley that August. Bourgeau, captivated by the mountain flora, stopped along the way to collect specimens. Hector pressed on to the old campground below The-Mountain-Where-the-Water-Falls (Cascade Mountain), to establish altitudes and do some mapping.

Reverend Robert Terrill Rundle, Protestant missionary in the North West Territories during the 1840s.

Doctor James Hector, physician and geologist on the Palliser expedition of 1857, which passed within 1,500 metres of the hot springs on Sulphur Mountain.

But the first geologist in the Bow Valley passed on without discovering its most interesting geological feature, the hot springs on Sulphur Mountain. He only missed this accomplishment by about 1,500 metres. The Cave and Basin springs were just across the river, hidden in the timber.

Imagine a conversation at some unseen crossroad between Heaven and the Big Sands. Two spirits rein in their painted horses, well met, for the last time.

"Nimrod, ye auld rascal!" cries one, "why did ye no tell me aboot the hot springs on yon mountain?"

"Huh, Doctor. Why ye no ask me?"

Near Castle Mountain, west of today's Banff, Nimrod lost control of Hector's destiny. In the name of that bugaboo, Curiosity, the party left the beaten track to push its way through terrain too miserable for mammals to inhabit. The hunting became steadily more desperate: their dried meat rotted and turned slimy in the rain. Pity the mountain explorer who starts out lost and stays lost until he finds himself again. Soaked at dawn, broiled at noon, and frozen at night, he finds nature too extreme to be trusted. But though her stock of deer may be depleted, her blood-sucking hordes of deer flies are fat and provocative. And as for the trails, they were mere suggestions: innuendoes among the wet, dripping trees, promises across the rockslides, tracery above the precipice, where Fate hung in the balance of a fly-crazed, footsore horse.

They were glad indeed when Nimrod finally shot a moose, and gladder still to meet a party of "throat cutters" who had killed six more of the "big deer." Hector, a veteran haggis eater, smacked his lips over the Indian delicacies: "moose nose and entrails, boiled blood and roast kidneys." After an orgy of eating and a good sleep, they were roused on the Sabbath morning by an aubade of blood-curdling Wesleyan hymns, sung loud enough to put the fear of God into man and beast alike.

After a few days of feasting and resting, Hector and his men left for the plains, provisioned with dried meat by the hospitable mountain people.

Just one year later, in 1859, the Stoneys were startled to see yet another party of hungry white men emerge from the timber in pursuit of a square meal. The Indians dusted off their hymns and made room around the stew pots for the Earl of Southesk, the first "tourist" to visit the Bow Valley. He and his crew had entered the valley from the north, via the Pipestone River, near Lake Louise. Southesk, a noted hunter, was in pursuit of the wily mountain goat, whose retiring ways had reduced his Lordship to a "sort of frenzy," as he put it.

In those days, no one travelled in the mountains merely for amusement: Southesk was unique, a kind of freak to White and Indian alike. But Southesk suffered much. In his quixotic questing, he had been bruised and lacerated by many a joust with the sinister deadfall that crowds every trail: "The smaller trees meet you like *chevaux-de-frises* placed at every angle . . . nothing but leather is a defense. I often felt as if in a tournament of old, as these lances of the forest splintered against my buff jerkin and nearly drove me out of the saddle or, artistically aimed at my head, lifted my 'beaver' off."

Being the first tourist, Southesk had a right to complain about the roads and the scenery. To him, majestic Cascade Mountain was "in no way remarkable." The Earl could have used a long soak in the hot springs to cheer him up, but nobody invited him. It's too bad: his Lordship was a good sport.

The few parties of white men came and went, but life in the valley went on much as it always had, hymns notwithstanding. Though the Stoneys kept the secret springs of Sulphur Mountain to themselves, something had been stolen from them nonetheless. It was knowledge; knowledge of the way the river ran, where the passes led, what lived in the stillness, what trees could be cut from the mountain-sides, what minerals could be mined from the rocks with picks and blasting powder.

The valley could now be described, partially at least, with Arabic numerals and English names: it was an entity, a thing that could be drawn on a map, and pic-tured in the mind. It was fated to be ignored for another quarter of a century, but it would not be forgotten. In time, it would be the lifeline of a new nation.

These Springs are Worth
A Million Dollars

On October 21, 1875, two American fur hunters reined up at a brand new trading post that was slowly taking shape on the Morleyville flats along the banks of the Bow River. Willard Burill Younge (or Peter Young, as he was generally known), and his partner Benjamin Pease had travelled up from Montana by covered wagon drawn by oxen. They were headed for the upper Bow River to trap and prospect, in the casual manner of American mountainmen of those days.

That Younge and Pease could meander at will across the plains in an ox-drawn wagon without being plundered shows how tenuous the Blackfoot hold on the country had become by 1875. Nearly half of Alberta's Indians had died in the smallpox epidemic of 1870. The pestilence was followed by a plague of hard case American whiskey traders pushing north across the boundary. For furs and buffalo robes, they offered an addictive liquid poison. "Firewater" was a mixture of pure grain alcohol, swamp water, chewing tobacco, red peppers and red ink.

With the arrival of the red-coated Mounties in 1874, the whiskey forts closed up shop almost overnight. Here and there around their gutted ruins, human skulls dotted the scorched earth.

But at Morleyville, where the Reverend George McDougall was building a mission, Younge and Pease found a small glimmer of Christian fellowship at the foot of the shining mountains. They stayed for a few weeks, and they traded their ox teams for saddle and pack horses to go into the mountains. While they were at the mission, something unprecedented occurred.

Pease, who could speak Sioux, struck up a conversation with some of the Stoneys. Perhaps he was generous with his tea and tobacco, or perhaps one of them just took a liking to him. At any rate, not only did he hear of the Cave and Basin hot springs, but his informant gave him some vague directions as to their location. When the two white men left Morleyville, they had already decided to ascend the south side of the Bow in search of the springs.

Prospecting along the way, they finally made the ford above Bow Falls around December 3. They worked their way through the timber west of today's Banff until they saw a tell-tale plume of steam rising above the shadowy spruce trees. This long delayed visit by the first Whites was anticlimactic in the extreme.

It seems that Younge and his partner didn't even bother to take a dip. In later

The whiskey trade was a dangerous business run by desperate men. From Fort Whoop-Up, near present-day Fort Macleod, in 1873 comes this footnote to a sad era of Alberta history, sent to a trader in Fort Benton, Montana:

Dear Friend:

My partner, Will Geary, got to putting on airs and I shot him and he is dead. The potatoes are looking well.
Your's truly,
Snookum Jim.

years Younge told a friend that "he made no claim for having discovered the springs, as he said the Indians used to take a wash in the Basin!" Early explorers have commented on the Stoneys' liking for daily bathing, whatever the weather. This predilection for cleanliness was not always shared by the white mountainmen, an odoriferous crew who bathed but seldom on the trail.

Younge built a cabin close by the ford on the Bow (near the present park administration building), where he and Pease spent the winter. Pease gave up his share in the springs after a season of trapping. Younge had a notion that the springs might be valuable someday, but lacked the money to register a claim. He left the valley in the summer of '76, and in his wanderings, tried to find investors to pay for a survey of the springs. As he told William Pearce, presiding Commissioner at the Hot Springs Inquiry of 1886, he was "always ridiculed" whenever he spoke of his find.

Poverty and hard luck dogged Younge's life. Not until 1885, when other white men were in residence at the Cave and Basin, did he find the means to hire counsel and assert his rights. By then it was too late, but his claim to be the original white discoverer is supported by eight affidavits sent to Ottawa by distinguished Alberta pioneers. George McDougall's testimony sums up the rest. He writes simply, "Younge and party were the first Whites to find the hot springs at Banff."

Younge made several trips to his shack after 1875. He was not in residence when Commissioner Pearce first came to the valley in 1884, but Pearce did see the shack. "It appeared to have been erected upwards of ten years previously," he later recalled. Younge's plan to return to the valley in 1885 was interrupted by the Riel Rebellion, in which he saw action as a trooper in Steele's Scouts.

The smoke from the first white resident's chimney was a signal that heralded a new era for the Bow Valley. Not that development proceeded at breathtaking speed for the next decade. There might have been more white visitors if Younge's story of the springs had reached more credulous ears. The commercial value of thermal water was well known to North Americans of Younge's era, exemplified in the famed resort at Hot Springs, Arkansas. The need to protect such valuable phenomena had resulted in the establishment of the world's first national park, Yellowstone, in 1872.

Destiny, deflected northward for so long by the fierceness of the Blackfoot nation, would catch up with the Bow Valley in her own sweet time.

In 1867, the nation of Canada had been born. A transcontinental railroad was the price demanded by British Columbia for union with the rest of the Dominion. In 1871 Prime Minister Sir John A. Macdonald had pledged to complete the rail link within ten years. To find a way across the mountains, he appointed a "mountain

Major A. B. Rogers, minus tobacco chaw.

of a man,'' Sandford Fleming, as Engineer-in-Chief of the Canadian Pacific Railway.

Businessmen and engineers had been tantalizing the public with plans for a continental railway, or a railway combined with canals, for over forty years. Lack of capital, and whimsical proposals such as Lieutenant Millington Henry Synge's system of locks to ascend the Rockies with ''steps of still water,'' proved to be the undoing of these dreamers.

Fleming, an author, explorer, engineer and scientist (he was the inventor of Standard Time), had the first feasible plan for the road. After a personal reconnaissance by steamer, boat, cart, horse, and Shank's Mare he had found the pass across the Rockies. It was to be the Yellowhead, one of the historic routes of the fur brigades, avoiding the southern plains, which Captain Palliser and others had found too arid for settlement.

All that changed very late in the game. In 1881, the construction of the railroad was signed over to a syndicate of international financiers. Professor John Macoun, botanist and explorer, convinced the CPR moguls that the southern prairies were far from arid. One day they would be the ''garden of the whole country,'' he asserted.

Good land meant faster settlement, and that meant faster profits for the railway. At a meeting in St. Paul, Minnesota in '81, the directors made a decision that would change the history of the northwest forever. The railway would go by way of the ''Bow Pass'' (they did not even know the name of the Kicking Horse Pass at the time!). As for the unexplored Selkirk Mountains beyond, well, a pass would just have to be located.

The man selected to survey a route up the Bow River and across the Selkirks had never heard of Willard Younge or his fabulous hot springs. Major A. B. Rogers missed the springs, as did the men who worked for him. They were kept too busy and too hungry to indulge in extracurricular explorations. Rogers himself was said to live mainly on chewing tobacco. An unending stream of it poured from between his batwing sideburns. His packers, axemen, and surveyors lived on bannock, beans, and salt pork. Anyone who asked for luxuries like butter or sugar was told, ''Blue Jesus man! You're making a god of your stomach!''

The Major's only hunger was his insatiable lust for fame. The CPR directors offered him a five thousand dollar bonus to find a pass across the Selkirks, and they promised that it would be named after him. Rogers found his pass, but he didn't cash his bonus cheque until a fussy accountant demanded balanced books, years later.

The Major was a stickler for details in surveying matters, but never stood on ceremony otherwise. His greeting upon first meeting his party chief in that land of great ups and downs was terse and to the point: "What's your altitude?" he snapped. The poor man didn't know. There followed a string of curses such as the mountains had never heard before. After that, the height above sea level was a popular topic of conversation throughout the working day.

By mid-summer of 1883, the end of steel had reached Fort Calgary, just 128 kilometres east of present-day Banff. The whistle of the first steam locomotive to enter the Rocky Mountains echoed and re-echoed among the high peaks of the Bow Valley that autumn. An army of labourers living in tent cities and hastily thrown-up shacks swarmed into the mountains. The air was blue with the smoke of campfires — and the multilingual profanity of hard-driven, track-laying teams. A

CPR line into Laggan, N.W.T. (now Lake Louise).

staccato chorus of sledgehammers startled the deer from the aspen forest. At night, defying prohibition, throats lubricated with smuggled moonshine lifted in a song to greet the risen moon:

> *For some of us are bums,*
> *For whom work has no charms,*
> *And some of us are farmers,*
> *A-working for our farms,*
> *But all are jolly fellows,*
> *Who come from near and far,*
> *To work up in the Rockies,*
> *On the CPR.*

A season of chaos descended on the Bow Valley. Wild fires, started by blasting or by runaway campfires, swept through the timber, blackening the mountainsides. Sir Sandford Fleming, brought out of retirement in England to inspect the route laid out by the eccentric Major Rogers, camped one night at Hillsdale, west of Banff Station. He was dismayed by the destruction and chilled by the sight of fires ''running up the mountainside . . . .gleaming with a weird light.''

Fleming was one of the few men whose mind could penetrate the haze of smoke and appreciate the mountain grandeur towering overhead. It was he who made the first proposal for a national park in Canada, in fact for two parks, one at Lake Superior and one in the mountains. His motive was far from altruistic. He saw the Rockies as another Switzerland, ''a source of general profit,'' especially for the CPR, which would carry the tourist traffic. In a few short paragraphs published in his book *England and Canada* (1884), Fleming predicted the kind of wealthy patrons such a park would attract, and mentioned the improvements, the bridle paths and ''retreats'' that would be needed for them. It was a small but accurate blueprint for the first park, whose birth was drawing very near.

Another powerful figure in Canada's history who came to the valley in 1883 was William Cornelius Van Horne, the CPR's fire-eating general manager. This burly tycoon had a gentler side. He was a gifted amateur artist, deeply impressed with the solitary splendor of the Rockies. Van Horne lingered at Lac Des Arcs, near today's Exshaw, to admire the November scenery, the trees and sandbars dusted with fresh snow.

Van Horne urged Commissioner William Pearce to recommend a park reserve around the lake, and told Pearce, ''if the suggested reservation was made, he would build a fine house on that island in the lake.'' According to Pearce, a survey was made, and the land duly reserved for a time, but as he explains in an unpublished memoir of the event: "The next time Van Horne saw the place . . . .a gale was blowing . . . . The result was that on account of clouds of dust, he could not see the lake or the island he had selected. It was a joke for some years in alluding to the place to call it Van Horne's Park."

Not long after his visit, either late in 1883 or early in 1884, Van Horne approved the name "Banff" for the locale near Siding 29. The story goes that the name came up at a CPR directors' meeting. Sir George Stephen, a board member, was born in Banffshire, Scotland, and director Donald Smith, another Scot, knew the area well. I like that name, said Van Horne. So the place was named, to the consternation of tourists ever since, who flounder over its double consonants with "Bimpf," "Ban-iff," "Bumf," and most entertainingly "Ban-fuh-fuh."

It was two great railwaymen who first envisioned a park in the Rocky Mountains, but three lowly CPR workers were about to make the discovery that would turn such whimsical notions into reality, only two years later. When work shut down for the winter of 1883, the end of steel was within a few kilometres of the Great Divide.

On November 8, three young easterners came up to the old campground below Cascade Mountain to do some sparetime prospecting. Franklin McCabe, 26, was a Nova Scotian, employed as section foreman at Padmore (Kananaskis). With him were two friends who had worked for him, William McCardell, 26, and William's younger brother, Thomas, both from Perth County, Ontario.

The three were intrigued by a queer-looking mountain (Sulphur Mountain, then known as Terrace Mountain) across the river. McCabe, a former coal miner, felt the mountain was worth exploring for minerals. It was a typical Banff November, too cold to swim and too warm to go skating; the river was still unfrozen. The three men built a crude raft and poled across the river at a point adjacent to the mountain's north ridge.

They beached their craft, and found themselves slogging through a cheerless swamp. As they moved up the boggy slope of the mountain, the water underfoot grew warmer. They exchanged surprised looks, and rushed forward to the foot of a yellowish bank. A strong smell of sulphur greeted them, and there, at the base of a small cliff, lay a large basin of steaming water, partly blocked with fallen timber.

In his unpublished memoirs, *Reminiscenses of a Western Pioneer*, the loquacious William McCardell describes their reaction to the startling find: "Our enthusiastic interest at this discovery was beyond the description of words. Our joyousness and the invigorating thrill we experienced in thus locating this strange phenomena, and hidden secret of the wilderness knew no bounds . . . ."

The McCardells and McCabe tromp through the swamp (From the N.F.B./Parks Canada film Steam, Schemes and National Dreams *with David Daniels, Steve Atkinson and Raimund Stamm).*

". . .a large basin of steaming water, partly blocked with fallen timber." (from Steam, Schemes and National Dreams.)

Opposite: William Cornelius Van Horne, CPR General Manager.

"We don't know what secrets of nature's treasures may be revealed in this spot." (From Steam, Schemes and National Dreams.)

Lowering the jack pine ladder (From Steam, Schemes and National Dreams).

After a brief and exciting time at the lower pool, the three men followed their noses up the bank and found the convoluted mouth of a cave opening, like the vent in a beaver lodge, on a treed terrace overlooking the valley. (That same steaming opening is visible today, protected by steel bars but otherwise unchanged.)

Silently, the three men knelt down to listen to the sound of the earth's innards gurgling in the darkness below.

When he wrote his account of the discovery, William McCardell was in his eighties, and his characters were moving on the long, frayed strings of memory. His most annoying, and at the same time humanly endearing trait, is the inflated rhetoric he puts in the mouths of McCabe, his brother, and himself. The three young workingmen are robbed of their reality at the most crucial moments. So, as the younger McCardell crouches by the dark hole of the cave, a cartoon balloon seems to float over his head as he turns to the eyes of history, and says stylishly: "We don't know what secret of nature's treasures may be revealed in this spot."

In his *Reminiscenses,* William tells of limbing off a "jack-pine" to serve as a ladder into the cave on the day of discovery. But in 1886, he told the Hot Springs Inquiry that his party had nothing but a knife with them on November 8, to carve their initials on some trees as first "discoverers" of the springs. William had to cut down a tree "about forty-five feet long" (over 13 metres) to reach the bottom of the cave. He was one helluva whittler was William.

At any rate, on a subsequent trip shortly after the discovery, the three did go into the depths, using a "jack pine ladder" and a safety rope. William, the first to descend, struck a match and saw "beautiful, glistening stalactites . . . like some fantastic dream of the Arabian Nights."

He was joined by brother Tom, who was awed into silence, but not for long: "I can't find words to give expression to my enthusiastic surprise," he lied. "It is a great sight and somewhat of an adventure also to come down into this wonderful and unknown, secret hidden world gleaming with treasures of old Mother Nature." As a former coal miner, McCabe knew a few tricks that that old harlot Mother Nature could play in the darkness of her underground sink holes. He waited until he was sure the cave was free of methane gas and surprise precipices before climbing down into the depths. McCabe was duly impressed with the "chamber of jewels" and "hidden . . . treasure," as he described it.

It was not sulphur the three men smelled as they stripped and plunged into the crystal pool for the first swim. Their nostrils flared to the invigorating scent of dollar bills. The stalactites gleamed like bars of silver and gold, the roof glittered as if studded with diamonds. There were thousands of navvies due to start work next spring, and hot water bathing was a luxury item along the CPR right-of-way. More importantly, the railroad would bring the wealthier set, and the hot springs would draw them like honey draws bees.

They set to work building a fence around the cave, to let other men know that this particular miracle had been pre-empted, and would be subject, some day, to an admission charge. It was a notion that would bring these first entrepreneurs bad luck, and cause a bitter rift between McCabe and his two happy-go-lucky pals.

Things went well at first. Led by McCabe, the boys made a circle of the mountain and discovered more hot springs; the Middle Springs, as they are now known. And later on that winter, Frank and Tom saw a plume of steam at the 1,500-metre level on Sulphur Mountain, marking the Upper Hot Springs. Following their directions, William claims that he discovered these springs on New Year's Day, 1884.

McCardell built a crude shack a few metres from the Cave vent that winter, where they could stay on their visits to the place. But then things started to go a bit sour. According to William, the federal government refused their application to homestead at the springs because there were no homestead rights in the mountains. And they couldn't make out a mineral claim because the government did not recognize hot springs as a mineral resource at that time. It was the old bureaucratic shuffle now known as "Catch 22." The real problem, though, was the fact that most of the terrain was unsurveyed, and the boys needed a grubstake to hire a surveyor at the going rate: fifteen dollars a day.

The partners had to split up to earn their beans. William went to work on the railway in British Columbia, McCabe continued his sectionman job, and Tom, who was to be a "silent partner" despite his verbosity in William's memoirs, would stay in residence at the springs to keep off claim jumpers.

In the spring of 1884, the tracklayers returned to the mountains to push the steel on down the Kicking Horse River. The Cave and Basin quickly became known to these men; it was a wild and woolly spa where you could get a bath with unlimited hot water in a time when hot running water was a rarity; apparently a free bath, which doesn't say much for the business acumen of Tom McCardell.

When Parks Canada archaeologists explored the site in 1982, they found a collection of liquor bottles, a number of cartridge cases from a variety of shooting irons and, oddly, a small assortment of buckles. Perhaps, it is a testament to a few brief seasons of drinking, shooting and naked hilarity on the slopes of Sulphur Mountain.

Young William McCardell was the brains of a very haywire little outfit. His absence from the valley proved disastrous to the partnership. A number of rascals, gamblers, and speculators were attracted to the mountains that summer by a silver

William McCardell.

The first exhilarating swim (From Steam, Schemes and National Dreams).

Silver City and Castle Mountain, ca.1885.

mining boom near Castle Mountain. A collection of log huts, tents, and claptrap saloons, known as Silver City, sprang up in short order. The only thing needed to make the name stick was the presence of silver, which had not yet been discovered. Some of the wiser denizens were looking further afield for their meal tickets. Their attention fell on McCabe, good-natured, tractable Frank McCabe.

William had instructed McCabe to "do your best with the springs" while he (William) was away. McCabe's idea of developing the claim was to cut as many of his new friends into the action as possible. According to William, who found out about Frank's deals far too late, Frank "got together a powerful aggregation of manpower, but none of the men had such a thing as capital. They were, however, plentifully endowed with keen enthusiasm and hope." Hope is a powerful stimulus, and with high hopes one David Keefe cut a trail to the Upper Hot Springs, directed there by Frank McCabe, and built a shack in 1884. He was closely followed by McCabe and another man who further beshacked the place later that winter.

In spring, a young speculator's fancy turns from thoughts of dollar bills to thoughts of more dollar bills. In their log shanties along the CPR right-of-way, or at card tables in the saloons of Silver City (where the silver was rapidly turning into copper and the smiles were turning into scowls), the "powerful aggregation" began to suffer from a kind of avaricious cabin fever.

Since McCabe and McCardell had yet to patent their claim to the various hot springs, some of the newcomers convinced themselves that they deserved a bigger slice of the pie. Roused into action by these mutterings, the torpid McCabe sent a letter to the Minister of the Interior on March 20, 1885. In it he applied for rights to the Cave and Basin Springs on behalf of himself and William McCardell. Poor McCabe, who would later be described as "either dishonest or illiterate" by his partner, gave the letter to a friend named Archie NcNeil for rewriting and mailing. McNeil, seeing a good thing in the making, added his name and that of one of his pals to the letter as claimants without McCabe's knowledge.

There followed a spate of furious epistolizing and swearing of affidavits, as one Theodore Siebring claimed rights to the Upper Hot Springs on March 27, and McCabe, learning of this, fired off testimonials on May 18 denouncing Siebring's claim and asserting his own right by prior discovery. Frank McCabe, who in fact was not along when William McCardell first visited the Upper Hot Springs, was weaving a very tangled web. To complicate it further, he had, as the *Reminiscenses* politely inform us, "contracted a very unsatisfactory matrimonial engagement, out of which he was very anxious to unravel himself." To make matters even worse, the marriage knot, or noose, that McCabe was dodging, was apparently dangled by none other than Theodore Siebring's sister!

Ottawa was not inclined to recognize any exclusive rights to the springs. Instead, the Dominion Land Agent was sent out from Calgary to find out what all the fuss was about. After slogging his way through the swamp and barking his shins climbing down the jack-pine ladder, the agent concluded that McCabe and McCardell might have the honour of discovery, but had done precious little to improve their claim.

Both the land agent and another visitor, P. Mitchell, a former Conservative M.P., immediately realized the value of the springs as a potential spa. Mitchell reported directly to Prime Minister Macdonald on the value of the site, as ''at least half a million of dollars.''

The well-known springs at Arkansas were controlled by the American government, and Mitchell recommended to Sir John A. that he should follow the same policy at Sulphur Mountain. This information was not lost on Macdonald, ever on the lookout for natural resources to feed the railroad, and Ontario industries. He filed the information away in his commodious brain; he would bring it to mind in just a few months' time.

A number of politicians appeared at the Cave and Basin that summer of '85, travelling on free railroad passes provided by the CPR. One portly politico waded through the swamp, puffed his way with stertorous breath up the terraces to the Cave and, after a good rest, attempted to descend the ladder. But he jammed in the narrow opening like a cork in a bottle. A couple of other visitors, hearing his cries for help, rushed up with a long pole which they worked down under his rump and then, with much grunting and effort, eventually popped him loose.

All this interest in the claim was gratifying to Tom McCardell, who was in residence intermittently at least, though he accomplished nothing by way of improvements. There was time during the long winter of '84-85 to look again at the cave ''gleaming with treasures,'' to rub the soot off the coal oil lamp while showing off the Cave's beauties to visitors, and to pray for a miracle, for a genie to appear with a big sack of bullion, because talk is cheap but whiskey costs money.

Early that summer a genie suddenly appeared, wrapped in a cloud of cigar smoke, and accompanied by suitable attendants in pin-striped suits. The grand pooh-bah of the Canadian Pacific Railway had the look of a man who can make dreams come true. Tom and Frank extolled the virtues of the springs and, fastening a rope around their guest's hulking frame, helped him to descend the crude ladder.

After a while they heard him ruminating around in the depths and, at length, he started back to the surface. The bowler-hatted, double-chinned head of William Cornelius Van Horne slowly emerged out of the earth and glowered up at them. There was a hush as the oracular mouth opened: ''These springs are worth a million dollars!'' cried Van Horne unabashedly. It was the greatest compliment he could give.

The grateful, befuddled partners must have thought their wish was about to come true. How were they to know that Van Horne meant a million dollars — not for them, but for the CPR.

No messenger arrived in the wake of Van Horne's visit with a cash offer for the springs. Instead, a steadily increasing number of crippled or diseased pilgrims, who had heard of the sulphurated hot springs via the railroad grapevine, began to limp in, to soak their rheumatic bones and ''marinate their hemorrhoids'' as one unkind writer has described such therapy.

One of the earliest, if not the first, of these ''miracle cures'' was effected for a man named Harry Jennings, whom McCardell claims was sent to the springs by his doctor in Helena, Montana. Jennings had a horrible case of eczema with running sores on his body. For three months he haunted the cave spring, bathing his body in the water from the exit stream, and living in a tent until he ''walked away as well as ever he was.'' Jennings was soon followed by one ''Rattle Snake Johnson,'' who was suffering from some kind of reaction to a rattler bite. After two months of washing in the same stream Jennings had used, he too went away ''rejoicing at his marvellous recovery.''

Kept apprised of the goings on at the springs, William McCardell was cheered by news of these cures, but disturbed to hear of Frank's deals with the ''powerful aggregation.'' He wrote Frank and urged him to ''hang onto the springs,'' until he could get back with some money earned from tie cutting.

Unknown to the McCardells, Frank was by now desperate to escape the mountains in a state of pristine bachelorhood. He needed only some funds to pay his passage. At this opportune moment, D. B. Woodworth, M.P. for Kings, Nova Scotia, appeared on the scene to visit his relatives at the ''Cascade Ranch.'' This enterprising gent heard about the springs, and was soon circling about the place with a view to feathering his own nest.

To McCabe, Woodworth looked like the golden goose who would stake his escape from the snares of matrimony, in return for the heated ponds on Sulphur Mountain. To Woodworth, McCabe must have looked like a prize pigeon, ready for the plucking. Frank would not recognize his visitor for a true bird of prey until he felt Woodworth's talons sinking into his neck.

On August 25, Woodworth wrote to the Minister of the Interior urging that McCabe's claim to the springs be given every consideration. It seems like a munificent request, except that Woodworth himself contrived to become the main beneficiary of it. On August 31, he registered his purchase of McCabe's and

McCardell's interest in the springs with the Dominion Land Agent in Calgary. Somewhere around the 25th of August, good old Frank had sold his partners down the river for the sum of $1,500.00. Then the ex-miner went to earth in Calgary, awaiting payment. But all he ever received was an I.O.U. and Woodworth's golden promises, unredeemable at the bank.

Meanwhile, back at the springs, Tom McCardell finally sniffed the wind of corruption above the stink of hydrogen sulphide. "Come at once," ran the message he telegraphed to his brother. "Important business concerning the springs."

William caught the first train east. The brothers were soon circling the little cluster of shacks and tents at Banff, trying to cut McCabe's trail. Woodworth tried to smooth things over with the McCardells at a meeting held in his relative's cabin. He promised William a share in the springs if he would "keep quiet," and tried to get him to admit that McCabe had the legal right to act on William's behalf. In the shadowy room, beyond the range of the coal oil lamp, one of Woodworth's cohorts lay hidden behind a curtain to gather "evidence" for Woodworth in case of legal problems later.

The ruse might have worked if Woodworth had offered some hard cash: William felt his share of the claim was worth at least ten thousand dollars and denied McCabe had sold anything but his own interest. But Woodworth offered only promises, while waiting official recognition for McCabe's rights to the spring. He was convinced that McCabe had power of attorney to act for William.

Someone let slip the news that Woodworth was heading east in a few days to meet with the Minister of the Interior, the Honourable Thomas White, who was then at Regina. Determined to track down McCabe and forestall Woodworth, the boys caught the next "rattler" for Calgary, and an interview with the Chief of Police, Jack Ingram. A warrant was sworn out for McCabe on a charge of forgery, and the boys fanned out to scout the pioneer town on the trail of the befuddled Nova Scotian.

At the Grand Central Hotel there was a letter box that served as unofficial post office where messages could be passed on. Thumbing through the papers there, William was delighted to find a sealed envelope addressed in McCabe's handwriting to "Mr. D. B. Woodworth, M.P." Ingram was soon on the scene, and opened the letter, which read:

> *For God's sake come at once and pay me some money. The money agreed to, as I am anxious to leave the country. And I am suffering the tortures of Hell in waiting here! I am in a shack six telegraph poles east of the Elbow Bridge.*

McCabe and the McCardells' first shack, beside the Cave vent.

"Come along, and we will get him in his hideout lair!" cried Ingram melodramatically.

Counting poles, the three men sleuthed down the telegraph line, located the shack, and collared the unfortunate McCabe. The cold hand of the law and William's hot tongue lashing chastened the frightened felon. He went along with William to see James A. Lougheed (grandfather of the present Premier of Alberta). Lougheed, "a young, red-blooded lawyer, full of fight," as William describes him, drafted a twenty-two dollar telegram to the Minister of the Interior in Regina. Woodworth received a shock a few days later when the Minister, the Hon. Thomas White, confronted him with the telegram. Both the McCardells and McCabe repudiated the sale of any rights to the crafty M.P.

Furious and embarrassed, Woodworth headed back East to lick his wounds, for the time being.

McCabe tried to patch things up that night by taking the brothers and Ingram out to dinner, treating them to wine and caviar. But later that evening, after confessing that he was stony broke with no money to help develop the springs, he got up and walked out into the night, full of remorse. "Frank feels real cheap," commented Tom, with a marked economy of adjectives.

McCabe's golden goose had been cooked by Lougheed's telegram. The three partners, one of them bound to the partnership by the threat of arrest, returned to the Cave and Basin to squat on their unrecognized claim.

Alexander Burgess, Deputy Minister of the Interior, was determined to reserve the springs for the government. The lead shown by the Americans in setting aside Yellowstone National Park and the Arkansas Hot Springs helped to guide his plans. Nobody had bothered to inform the partners as yet. But other men, closer to the seat of power in Ottawa, already knew the fate of the springs, in that time when politics and big business slipped in and out of the same set of clothes, as occasion suited them.

Officials returning from Banff that summer seemed to have brought a whiff of sulphur or the scent of lucre back with them to the capital. One entrepreneur, one of many who lifted his muzzle to the political breeze that August, was Ottawa lawyer McLeod Stewart. On August 29, he applied to the Minister of the Interior for a ninety-nine-year lease on the entire Banff Springs area. He graciously offered to assume control providing that "before a lease is granted to myself and assigns for the land, at least $50,000 must be expended on the erection of buildings for the accommodation of visitors and construction of roads, tramways, bridges, bridle paths, and other improvements."

A national park had not yet been proposed in parliament, and the people had no conception of what the purpose of such a park might be. The speculators alone saw the thing clearly: it was to be a private preserve for the protection of investments and the propagation of dollar bills.

Stewart's whole application was conditional on the lands at Banff being "set aside and forever reserved as a national park." This cheeky speculator also seems to be the first man on record to propose the name "Banff National Park" for the springs area. Stewart was obviously privy to some inside information on the government's plans.

The Prime Minister effectively settled the future of the springs on October 16 in a note to Burgess, in which he expressed a hope that "great care had been taken to reserve all the land in or near the Hot Springs at Banff. No squatting should be allowed," he wrote, "and any attempt to squat should be resisted."

It remained for the Minister of the Interior to visit the site, which he did in October. He found the McCardells still in residence, and soon let them know that no rights of ownership would be allowed for the springs, though some compensation might be paid to the partners for their "improvements."

McCardell described White as a "fine fellow" though "his opinion as to McCabe having set the price on the springs through his fraudulent sale to Woodworth was not inspiring to Tom and myself." McCabe, lurking in the bushes behind the shack, kept out of sight while his uninspired partners were discussing his virtues.

White, on the other hand, was not impressed with the trio, or with the rest of the powerful aggregation. "It would be a great misfortune," he wrote to the Prime Minister on November 21, "to permit the springs to get into the hands of any of these claimants." White detailed William Pearce, Superintendent of Mines and general trouble shooter for the Dominion Lands Branch, to draw up a description of the proposed reserve area, amounting to a little more than twenty-six square kilometres on the north-facing slopes of Sulphur Mountain. It was submitted to Privy Council. And on November 28, 1885, the world's third national park (after Yellowstone National Park and Royal National Park in Australia), and Canada's national park system, began, inauspiciously, when Order-In-Council No. 2197 was approved. The enabling clause reads:

> His Excellency by and with the advice of the Queen's Privy Council
> for Canada has been pleased to order, and it is hereby ordered,
> that whereas near the station of Banff on the Canadian Pacific
> Railway, in the Provisional District of Alberta, North West Ter-
> ritories, there have been discovered several hot mineral springs
> which promise to be of great sanitary advantage to the public,
> and in order that proper control of the lands surrounding these

William Pearce, the ''Czar of the West.''

springs may be vested in the Crown, the said lands in the territory including said springs and in their immediate neighbourhood, be and they are hereby reserved from sale or settlement or squatting.

It is sobering to think that the world's largest national park system, with its sublime array of mountains, lakes, tundra, forest, prairie and sea shores began with such a homely reference to its ''sanitary advantage.'' The Stoneys had thought of the springs as a sacred place, an abode of beneficient spirits. The white fathers of the nation seemed to regard their first national park reserve as a gigantic sitz bath!

There is a kind of typically Canadian embarrassment exemplified here, the inability to admire great landscapes without somehow attaching a dollar value. We have changed enough over the years to deplore such philistinism, but it seems unlikely that the national park idea would have taken root so early in our history without the two key elements of transportation (the railroad) and a potential hot springs spa (a market for the railroad). There was little aesthetic enthusiasm for wilderness in the Great Lone Land of the northwest, which was one vast stretch of wilderness punctuated by the lights of isolated villages and farms.

Thanks to Frank McCabe and the McCardells, the government had been pushed into establishing the first national park reserve. A small stampede of squatters moved in to try and establish rights on this potential money maker. The government dispatched William Pearce to Banff to send them packing, and to erect signs forbidding construction without permission of the Minister of the Interior in ''Banff Springs Park,'' as it was briefly known. But those who had arrived prior to November of 1885 demanded payment for their ''improvements.'' The Minister appointed Pearce to hold a hearing, known as the Hot Springs Inquiry, to settle the various claims.

Pearce had a solid reputation as an arbiter in land disputes. He had earned it in Manitoba settling Metis land claims, when the only survey instrument previously used was the curved belly of a horse lined up with the horizon to show the back boundary of the lot. Pearce had an encyclopedic knowledge of the land in Western Canada and in the mountains he knew every stand of marketable timber along the length of the CPR. This cranky Victorian gentleman was hard to travel with. His son William ''Buck'' Pearce remembers one trip across the Prairies with his father. Every mile or so, the old man would demand: ''What township are we in now? Which section? Which quarter section?'' Pearce Senior knew the answers within a few acres. As an inspector of land agencies, Pearce had sweeping powers to settle disputes on the spot, to reserve land from settlement, and to devise policies for lumbering and mining development. He was known, quite appropriately, as the ''Czar of the West.'' The Sulphur Mountain hot springs had not escaped his scrutiny, either.

He first saw the Cave in September of 1885. The row kicked up by McCardell and McCabe late that summer had aroused his curiousity. Pearce, a bluff looking frontiersman used to hiking when no other transportation was available, didn't identify himself to the men at the hot springs. It appears he was treated rudely, regarded as somewhat of a nuisance, a sort of visiting clodhopper. The McCardells, McCabe, David Keefe, and assorted cronies were hanging about the place, no doubt celebrating their rout of the recalcitrant Woodworth. They were young men, and a trifle full of themselves, with big fish to fry — or so they thought. No one would guide Pearce to the Upper Springs or to Lake Minnewanka. He was told, curtly, that he could not find either place by himself. The big man merely smiled, and went on his way. The wilderness was an open book to William Pearce. He was used to finding his own way through it.

"These things are mentioned," he writes in his unpublished memoir of the event, "as they stood me in good stead when later I had to report on the alleged discovery of these springs, and the promotion of them by the claimants for remuneration, for the alleged service." It must have afforded Pearce a laugh up his sleeve when he saw the expressions on those faces at the opening of the Hot Springs Inquiry in 1886. The man they had treated so shabbily was now sitting in judgment on their claims.

David Keefe, one of the applicants, might talk about the "access" he had provided across the Bow River for visitors to the springs, but Pearce knew exactly what the "access" was. "It consisted of a few ties lashed together by telegraph wire forming a raft, both ties and wire being owned by the Canadian Pacific Railway." Pearce awarded Keefe one hundred dollars.

There was not much point in McCardell going on at great length about "improvements" either. Pearce had climbed down the same jack-pine ladder that William had installed in 1883. In the end, more as a gesture of goodwill than anything else, he awarded William and Frank the sum of $675 each for their time at the springs, the springs that Van Horne had valued at a million dollars.

But first, poor McCabe was grilled by all parties as thoroughly as any smoked herring from his native Maritimes, as Woodworth tried to justify his own claim, and Lougheed tried to refute it. Woodworth was in the bizarre position of having to prove that the hostile McCabe had acted honourably, to thus dignify Woodworth's own sharp practices.

"I don't know how the law runs!" cried the exasperated McCabe at last, "I don't carry as much law as you do!" He told Commissioner Pearce: "I asked him (Woodworth) several times for the money and he did not give it to me, and when he was going away I asked him to give me the document back, and he said not to bother him, that he was sick."

The bemused Commissioner watched as Woodworth was slowly "hoisted by his own petard." The M.P. had demanded $4,397 for his efforts at building some trails near the springs, and for a shack purchased at Silver City, which was to have been set up as a "hotel." Pearce wanted to settle matters quickly. He awarded Woodworth one thousand dollars and suggested if that wasn't to his liking, that he would be glad to charge him with trespassing on Crown Lands, destruction of timber, and damage to public property.

The politician blustered and fumed at Pearce's offer. Nervily, he told the Commissioner that the evidence concerning him should never have been revealed. It was "prejudicial to his status as a public man." Obviously, he believed his actions were a normal part of the political code of his day and no one seems to have seriously challenged them. Woodworth didn't deign to put himself on the witness stand. He packed his carpet bag and left the hot springs for good.

Other claimants received nothing. Siebring's claim was dismissed on the grounds that the eyesore he had erected at the Upper Hot Springs was not an improvement to the site. One man who had his eye not on money but on posterity was Joe Healy, who made no request for compensation, but claimed to have discovered the Upper Hot Springs and the Cave and Basin in 1874. Healy had nothing but his word for proof. In the atmosphere of general prevarication that surrounded the Inquiry, one man's word counted for little.

Willard Younge, who had the best claim as first discoverer, was the last witness to testify. He had done nothing to develop the springs in the intervening years since 1875, and his claim to the springs was denied. He had been destitute for most of the period, and arrived back on the scene too late to assert his rights effectively. Pearce had made it clear that the government saw no intrinsic value in discovery alone, nor did Pearce identify the first white man to see the springs. Hot springs, like the wilderness in general, were of no real value in the primitive state; the value lay in the "improvement" or as we say today, in the "development" of them.

What the country needed was settlement, commerce, and markets; "improvement" on the largest possible scale. Everything depended on the success of the railroad; the political future of Sir John A. Macdonald, the fortunes of the great capitalist manufacturers, and the future of the country were all tied irrevocably to the iron road. That a national park reserve was founded in 1885 in such an atmosphere of fortune hunting, and at a moment when the nation had nearly foundered on the rock of Louis Riel, was not so much a measure of its founders' far-sightedness as it was an act of divine providence, from our point of view. The springs, once the peace ground of an ancient mountain people, then the fenced off, jealously guarded claim of a few speculating white men, were now to be the resort of all the people, set, as Sir John A. Macdonald described it, in a "nation's park."

On a sultry day in July of 1886, Lady Agnes Macdonald fell in love with a steam engine. It happened near romantic Lake Louise, discovered in 1882. There, near the station, Lady Agnes first set her eyes on the tall, dark and handsome locomotive that was to take the Prime Minister's train over the Great Divide.

Overcome with emotion, Lady Agnes made up her mind to swap her upholstered seat indoors for a wooden candlebox set by the engine's great cyclopean eye. She climbed madly up onto the cowcatcher, and refused all entreaties to return to earth. "Mr. E.," a railroad superintendent, was ordered to accompany her as bodyguard and chaperone.

"No good will come of it," muttered an obscure local yokel, of the kind that history generally ignores.

In defiance: "This is lovely . . . quite lovely! I shall travel on this cowcatcher from summit to sea!" And dang me, hang me, if she wasn't as good as her word (according to an article she herself penned for *Murray's Magazine* the following year).

The affair began with a tempestuous plunge down along that depraved torrent, the Kicking Horse River. "For a second only I feel a quickening of the heart pulse," she wrote torridly, "and a hot colour mounts to my face. But it is gone in a moment, and I am none the worse for that 'spurt' at the rate of fifty miles an hour."

Flying on through a brushfire with head bent and skirts closely gathered, the flushed and excited lady was perhaps the most singular bowsprit the Canadian Pacific Railway ever set upon a mountain engine. She was quite a change from the moose antlers that decorated some of them, trophies previously owned by moose who challenged the CPR for right-of-way, and lost. Her ride was not without danger. At one point, the cowcatcher caught a slow-moving pig and turned it into flying porkchops, which narrowly missed splattering Mr. E.

Somewhere down on the Thompson River (riding alone by then), Lady Agnes scared hell out of two English canoeists who had just climbed the railroad embankment to make a portage near the mouth of a tunnel. It was a wet tunnel with rivulets of water pouring from its roof. When the train sailed out into the light, the first thing they saw was Lady Agnes, pasted to the cowcatcher as if snatched up in the midst of some ethereal crosswalk, her long skirts flowing in the breeze, her oilskin coat flapping round her ankle boots, and lofting over her tresses — its black peak still streaming water — an umbrella; yes, a veritable bumbershoot.

Lady Agnes Macdonald.

The Kicking Horse Canyon, site of Lady Macdonald's "tempestuous plunge."

Sir John A. and Lady Agnes pause on their trans-continental train journey.

Of course since she had "not been introduced," decorum only allowed Lady Agnes a "solemn little bow" to the lads as she flashed out of sight.

That rude and practical man Van Horne had declined the Governor-General's offer of a silver spike for the tie to bind the nation at Craigellachie, as Pierre Berton has recorded in his book *The Last Spike.* It would be "as good an iron one as there is between Montreal and Vancouver, and anyone who wants to see it driven," said Van Horne, "will have to pay full fare." Something symbolic was needed to crown this achievement.

Why not Lady Agnes? Rampant on a cowcatcher, an ornament of triumphant empire, she trammels the pagan mountains with iron wheels moaning beneath her petticoats.

They knew how to travel in those days; but it was a leisurely trip even by Victorian standards. They stopped the train for lunch, pulled off to see the sights, dallied on the sidings for tea, and parked for the night to sleep. Lady Agnes took her tea on the cowcatcher, enthroned upon her candlebox. Sir John A. did ride for awhile beside his wife, but eschewed tea for a stronger tonic which he sipped in the comfort of his private car. He tended to ignore *l'affaire locomotive,* which he described as "rather ridiculous."

Sir John A. Macdonald.

The Prime Minister had much to ponder. The country was plunged into recession, and Canadians were not flocking West in droves as he had planned but were leaving in herds, as usual, for the States. Nova Scotia was threatening to pull out of Confederation, Quebec was still alienated over the martyrdom of Louis Riel, sacrificed to appease the pink-cheeked Orangemen of Ontario, and there was an election in January to be won. It was enough to drive a man to drink.

The railway was built and its stocks were beginning to rise, but it could not survive long without passengers and freight. The homesteaders would come eventually. In the meantime, it was to the moneyed classes, the nouveau riche of industry and the wealthy aristocrats of the old world, that Macdonald and Van Horne turned for customers. "Since we can't export the scenery," Van Horne declared, "we'll have to import the tourists," and Macdonald agreed.

Van Horne began the tradition of advertising "our mountains," as the Canadian Pacific liked to think of them, all around the world. At the same time, the CPR began building hotels in the mountains, providing luxurious lodgings at Field, B.C. (Mount Stephen House), and at the summit of the Rogers Pass (Glacier House).

Van Horne had a hotel and other things in mind for Banff. His plans called for rapid development of the "million dollar" hot springs. The CPR quickly arranged for a chemical analysis of the thermal waters. There was lots of "brimstone," known to the ancients for its curative properties. Other beneficial minerals included chlorine, calcium, magnesium, bicarbonate, sodium, potassium, and lithium.

With such promising reports of the health value of the waters, the Minister ordered an immediate survey of the reserve. He was anxious to get going on "improvements" like roads and bridges, which would "make of the reserve a creditable National Park," as he explained in his annual report for 1886.

Back from a fact-finding trip to Arkansas Hot Springs came Department Secretary John R. Hall. His news was not good. He'd found the attendants ignorant, the plumbing mutinous and the equipment frowzy with age and neglect. "A person suffering only from rheumatism," he complained, "may enter a tub immediately after it has been vacated by someone afflicted with a contagious disease." Hall recommended absolute government control over the springs at Banff, and management under medical supervision. That was too expensive to implement. Instead, the government imposed strict regulations for leasing the Upper Hot Springs, and opted for a government facility at the Cave and Basin.

As owner of the springs, the government found itself in the peculiar position of leasing hot water at fifteen dollars per tub, per annum. Two hotel-bathhouses, one built by Dr. R. G. Brett, a medical supervisor for the CPR, and one by partners Whitman and McNulty, would be licensed on this principle and built in the fall of 1886.

50

At Banff, George Stewart, Dominion Land Surveyor and landscape architect, was seconded from his surveying duties to act as the first superintendent early that summer. Stewart, operating out of a tent pitched at Banff Station, was just the kind of hard-driving developer the park reserve needed to "make a creditable National Park," as his superiors had put it.

The park reserve was, in fact, a mess, and the railroad was the unwitting architect of its destruction. The tie cutters had left acres of stumps; dynamiters and hunters had decimated the fish and game, and fires had obliterated a good deal of the remaining forest. In the Bow Valley, acres and acres of charred snags alternated with stands of lodgepole seedlings.

Earlier, Stewart had reported to the government on some relatively untouched country adjacent to the Bow Valley which he felt should be added to the park reserve. The Minister ordered him to include all points of interest "within reasonable bounds," and sent W. F. Whitcher, formerly Dominion Commissioner of Fisheries, to report on game and fish stocks in the area. His report, which would influence the parks policy for many years, is notable for its Victorian notions about wildlife and wildlife management.

George Stewart, first Superintendent of Rocky Mountains Park.

Despite the destruction of game and fish stocks, Whitcher still favoured sport hunting in the park, with an eye to the revenue this would bring in. However, the original people of the Bow Valley were to have no hunting rights at all. "Those who now invade that territory," he wrote, "are stragglers and deserters from their own reserves, where they are well cared for in food and clothing at the public expense." Whitcher's comment makes grim reading, when compared to the historic record. The Indians of his day were in a wretched, half-starved condition, due to the extinction of the great buffalo herds by about 1881.

He was similarly uninformed about, though more benevolently inclined towards, the park black bears and grizzlies, inventing a non-existent species based on colour variation. "Bears are of three kinds," he reported, "grizzly, cinnamon, and black," and he added with unintentional humour, "they generally protect themselves." "Not being habitually carnivorous, but rather vegetarian feeders, they need not be wantonly killed," he advised, "nor dealt with as we should do with the lupine, vulpine, and feline vermin that prey upon furred and feathered game with savage impartiality."

It seems that Whitcher had never heard of Darwin's theory of natural selection (survival of the fittest). To many Victorians, animals were divided into categories of "good" and "bad." Whitcher had a long list of animals to be rendered extinct in the reserves, including wolves, coyotes, foxes, lynxes, skunks, wildcats; in fact, just about any creature that preyed on other creatures. (Speculators, unfortunately, were not on his list.) Whitcher recommended a museum of natural history for Banff, so that "the mammal species so weeded out could be utilized in a satisfactory manner." The former fish inspector had a very utilitarian sort of mind.

The Minister of the Interior, less sanguinary than Whitcher, declined to order the extermination of that much interesting fauna, though it would not be until 1890 that hunting was totally prohibited in the park. In the Rocky Mountains Park Act of 1887, he would reserve his right to make laws for "the preservation and protection of game and fish, and of wild birds generally." The superintendent had, and still has, the authority to destroy any predator deemed hazardous to the public.

Whitcher had one enlightened recommendation, for the appointment of forest rangers "of which force, picked Indians would form a part." But no effective force was formed. As a result, Stewart found it impossible to protect the park wildlife during his term in office. At the outset, wildlife was of secondary importance to the park-makers of 1886.

Van Horne was on the prod, anxious to begin construction on the Banff Springs Hotel. The bathhouse builders were pressing the government to build roads. There was no bridge over the Bow, no road from the railway to the river. With government funds to hire the plentiful supply of ex-railroaders in the area, Stewart soon had several gangs in action. They levelled, chopped, shovelled, and graded their way to the river late that spring. His men paused to wipe the sweat off their brows, and fell to building a pontoon bridge across the Bow. In six days they floated it into position, crossed the river, dropped their hammers and picked up their axes again.

By the beginning of July, a road suitable for carriages was built to the Upper Hot Springs. By July 15, Stewart pushed his road to the lower springs. At the Cave, the irresistible forces of the doughty Stewart ran into some immovable objects in the form of William McCardell and his partners. As usual, money was the problem. Woodworth had received his thousand dollars but the "discoverers" had yet to get a penny.

Stewart planned to construct a spiral staircase down through the cave opening, and politely asked the troublesome trio to take a hike. McCardell, who like Stewart was of a Celtic turn of mind, quite wisely refused to move until the government paid up.

Short on time, but long on dynamite, Stewart decided against the spiral staircase and descended the hill. He suggested to his foreman that if one can't go over something, one might go under it. He drew a fast sketch for a tunnel to follow the existing stream from the cave, and left his men to blast and chisel their way under McCabe's and McCardell's claim.

At this juncture [McCardell floridly notes], things had reached a climax that was most important so far as us having any rights or claims were concerned. We would not be halting nor disturbing matters of Government movements, were we to sit placidly by and let the Government ignore us completely. So, it was decided to go down and stop the work of the tunnel, either by plain persuasion or kind entreaties. One of these methods was to be brought into play.

Whether by application of blarney or the laying on of shillelaghs, the upshot was that ''the men put on their coats and . . . left the job.''

The trio quickly received written assurances from the Minister of the Interior that they would be ''amicably settled with,'' and allowed the tunneling operation to proceed. In his *Reminiscenses,* McCardell claims that Stewart's tunnel destroyed many of the stalactites in the cave, and created a cold draft of air which lowered the temperature of the water supply. The blasting no doubt rattled the frying pans on McCardell's table as well.

The partners signed a quit claim that summer (McCardell calls it a ''quick claim'') sent by the government along with the pay-off. With that, they sadly left the scene of their speculations and daydreams.

Stewart left a crew at the springs to tunnel on through the winter. He put other men to work building a road from the bridge to the Banff Springs Hotel site. By the fall of that year, two bathhouses were in operation at the Upper Hot Springs. These were a great benefit to some unfortunates who came to the springs, not for pleasure but for mere relief from pain. Limping to the baths, or carried there in chairs or litters, these pimpled, poxed and palsied sufferers thronged Whitman's boarding house and Brett's Grand View Villa. At Brett's, they plunged into a log-lined pool, chinked with oakum. Some preferred to stew in an older mud-bottomed pool nearby, feeling the stinking gumbo there had rare medicinal qualities.

They soaked their gout-swollen joints in the steaming waters, and perhaps glanced askance at a bather furtively applying a poultice of muck to a suspicious-looking blemish. The sulphur water was touted as a cure for many diseases, including syphilis, that ancient curse of the hasty lover. Those dyspeptic and hypochondriac visitors who came to sip and gargle the nectar, rather than soak in it, did so, one assumes, upstream from the baths. In a world without our modern wonder drugs, medicinal hot springs offered a real, if only temporary, relief from pain and affliction. The 160 steps that led from the road up to the bathhouses had, in later years, a handrail made of crutches, left behind by those who had been ''cured'' of their ailments.

The Minister of the Interior was well satisfied with Stewart's efforts of 1886

and 1887. He had accomplished a very great deal in a very short time, to "make a park" in difficult circumstances of a brief summer season and a hard winter with deep snow. The government of the day did not regard virgin wilderness as the essential ingredient of a park. It had to be improved with roads and facilities and made accessible, "made useful" as Macdonald would have said, to the public first. And the Bow Valley, in its devastated state, did not qualify as wilderness anyway. However, there were to be tracts of wild forests and waterways in the larger area that Stewart had surveyed in 1886, which, when added to the park area, would enlarge it to 673.4 square kilometres.

In April of 1887, the government introduced a bill to formally create the national park which had in fact been in existence since November of 1885. They needed a set of regulations for the administration of the park and, not incidentally, they needed approval for the money that had already been spent.

The Prime Minister was the most eloquent champion on behalf of Rocky Mountains Park, as it was now to be known. He painted a glowing picture of how the mountain scenery would attract visitors from all around the world, bringing prestige and currency to Canada. "I have no doubt," he said with conviction, "that it will become a great watering place." The hot springs' water would "recuperate the patients" and the rental of the waters would "recoup the Treasury."

Sir John A. did not intend the reserve to be a mere humble resort for hoi polloi, however. "The doubtful class of people" (meaning the poorer classes) would not find a welcome in Banff. Instead, the villa lots that had been surveyed on the south bank of the Bow were to be "leased out to people of wealth, who will erect handsome buildings upon them."

Several M.P.s argued against this undemocratic line of thought. But few working people had the means to indulge themselves in intercontinental travel in that era, anyway. The opposition did object strenuously to the government's undertaking to "prepare hotels for tourists," and thereby benefit the CPR, which was already heavily funded by the Canadian taxpayer to the tune of seventy to eighty million dollars. "If the Government has grounds up there which can be made into convenient parks for public resorts for the wealthy people," cried one honourable member, "let them leave to individuals the business of doing so!"

A far from disinterested party, M.P. Donald Smith, defended the CPR's involvement at Banff and told the house that the corporation was building a hundred-thousand-dollar hotel there. Straining Parliament's never-generous sense of credulity to the limit, he said the hotel would be built not "as a matter of profit." Instead, when it had been made successful, it would be given over "on the most reasonable terms to those who will manage it properly, and make it a place of resort equal to any on the continent."

Opposite: Opening of Dr. R. G. Brett's Grandview Bathhouse, 1886. Dr. Brett is at far left on lower stairway landing.

The Honourable Mr. Casey accused the government of casting a "haze of poetry" over their fabulous hot springs, to obscure the expenditures made there. He characterized one Tory speech, made by an "honourable friend from the wild west," as being "the incarnation of the Banff Springs, namely, gush and gas."

The Prime Minister defended the government's involvement in the reserve. The government had a responsibility to make the reserve "useful" for the country, not just for the CPR. To make the park a showplace for the country, and superior to the Arkansas spa, it was clear that the government must regulate and administer the park. Yet coal mining and lumbering were to be allowed in the new park, and the government saw no contradiction between these activities and the enjoyment of the park by the public.

At least one honourable member, more farsighted than the rest, objected to industry in the park. He told Macdonald, "You cannot have a public park, with all the wild animals preserved in it, and have . . . trade and traffic involving railways going to and from the mines. If you intend to keep it as a park, you must shut out trade, traffic and mining."

He was absolutely right from our point of view, but too far ahead of his time to be listened to. In Macdonald's view, the national park was just another resource to be made use of in line with his own National Policy for the extraction and marketing of raw materials. "There may be places," he allowed, "where the property may be used for industrial purposes without interfering with the beauty of the park as a whole."

Macdonald out-argued his opponents, few of whom seriously disputed the creation of the park in principle. Fifty-fifty-one Victoria, Chapter 32, "An Act Respecting the Rocky Mountains Park of Canada," was given royal assent on June 23, 1887. The original notion of the park reserve being of "sanitary benefit to the people" was kept on in the opening clause of the Act, which described it as a "national park and sanatorium." The legislators of 1887 employed much the same phrases the Americans had used in dedicating Yellowstone National Park. It was "reserved and set apart as a public park and pleasure ground for the benefit, advantage, and enjoyment of the people of Canada."

Macdonald had slapped the infant park on the back in 1885 and presided over its coming of age in 1887. His expectations of his prodigal creation were very high, however. He demanded that it should pay its own way and "recoup the Treasury" from the very start. It had come into being already girded with a belt of iron that threatened its very existence and scarred it forever. More important, he had curbed its savage nature, and tried to make of it a civilized "pleasure ground" in the midst of a wilderness. And yet everything he had done was in the best interests of his nation and his culture at that time.

Opposite: Upper Hot Springs, ca.1888.

In the eastern United States, where industrial growth and devastation were decades ahead of Western Canada, writers like Thoreau and Emerson had epoused the mystical virtues of the vanishing wilderness before the middle of the Nineteenth Century. The desire to preserve some part of the wilderness was a central motif in the founding of Yellowstone Park. One of Yellowstone's advocates, Cornelius Hedges, expressed it thus: "This great wilderness does not belong to us. It belongs to the nation. Let us make a public park of it and set it aside . . . never to be changed but to be kept sacred always."

Yet the founders of Rocky Mountains Park could not have been inspired by the way this wilderness philosophy was interpreted by the U.S. government in Yellowstone. For fourteen years that park suffered official neglect. In 1886, the U.S. Army moved into the park to stop the wholesale destruction of lands and wildlife that had been going on ever since the park's inception.

Squatters had moved in and erected buildings, poachers were shooting buffalo and selling the heads at three hundred dollars each. Ranchers drove their cattle in to forage on the public domain. The stagecoaches carrying tourists to the park were sometimes held up by bandits, or shot up by fugitive bands of Bannock and Nez Perce Indians. Everyone, it seems, wanted a piece of the action. It's true that no railroad had yet desecrated the world's first national park. That was not through want of trying, in the early years at least, but through a bad economy for railroading.

Looking at the American experience, Canadian legislators tried to frame an act that would make the reserve a commercial success, but save it from the abuses of the ignorant and the avaricious. And while there were no homilies on the value of wilderness in the Act, one very important word was used in connection with the minister's power in 1887: the word "preservation," which shows that the lessons of the past were not entirely lost on our forefathers.

Clause 4(a) provides for the "care, preservation, and management of the park . . . watercourses, lakes, trees, and shrubbery, minerals, natural curiosities and other matters." Clause 4(f) gave the minister the power to make regulations for the "preservation and protection of game and fish, and of wild birds generally."

Here at least was the germ of the idea that is so central to our concept of conservation and of what national parks should be in our time.

Ultimately, we can't judge the actions of the park-makers of 1887 by the standards of our own age. The first park was shaped by the standards of its time and has been shaped by changing values ever since. Now that preservation is a cardinal virtue, we can only thank these ancestors for their efforts in setting the park aside, and, in shaping the parks of our own time, try harder to anticipate the needs of those who follow us up this same difficult trail to the future.

A Garden In the Wilderness

*I*f you fired a cannon down Banff Avenue in the spring of 1887, you might have conceivably killed somebody's cow, the cannonball otherwise flying on unhindered until it struck Cascade Mountain. Cows would soon be prohibited from grazing on the main street, or on the other four surveyed streets of the new town. Most people were too busy that spring swinging hammers to notice the livestock. The Canadian Pacific Railway's Banff Springs Hotel was under construction, and Dr. Brett had a crew working on his Sanitarium Hotel, sited where the park administration building now stands. Teamsters and livery operators were erecting stables and the lumber yard out at Banff Station was doing a roaring trade. The general store and the butcher shop were still located in the old town out at the station. There was even a furniture store, in case anybody found time to sit down and wanted to buy a chair.

George Stewart seemed to sit down only when he was in the saddle in the first hectic years of the park. He had moved, with his assistant John Connor, to a log shack near the Bow River that they had to share with the village's first school children during the week. The ringing of the teacher's hand bell every morning was the signal for Stewart to saddle up and get on his rounds. Park Inspector Connor, who was also fire and game warden and head clerk, had some paperwork to do most days, and sometimes found himself standing irritably at attention by his desk while the urchins sang *God Save the Queen*. "Now children, let's try it once more with some enthusiasm! Perhaps you would care to join in, Mr. Connor?"

As Stewart urged his horse through the muck and cow flop of Banff Avenue, headed for the Cave and Basin one day that spring, he was making mental notes for half a dozen projects that needed his attention. His horse's shod feet echoed on the swaying deck of the pontoon bridge, and he sourly eyed the high water sweeping between the floats. The abutments for a permanent iron bridge were now ready and, as soon as the material arrived, he would start construction. He had kept sentries on the floats through part of the winter, after a runaway boom of logs had nearly wiped out the fragile structure. The thunder of Bow Falls a few hundred metres downstream underlined the importance of the job: it was not safe enough. If it should break with a wagonload of tourists on it — he shook off the thought for now. And there was the Sanitarium, taking shape very fast. Probably too fast.

"Good morning," he greeted the foreman. What the devil was the fellow's name again? People come and go so fast these days.

"Ah. Top o' the mornin' to ye, Sor."

Hmm. Obviously a Mick-Something. "I see you have the pipes now for your baths."

"Aye, that we do."

"I also see that they are entirely too light. Did Dr. Brett not get my message then?"

"Now what message might that be?"

The Superintendent sighed with exasperation. His crews were building several

"If you fired a cannon down Banff Avenue in 1887, you might have conceivably kill-ed somebody's cow."

thousand metres of pipelines, carried in moss-lined boxes, to supply the Banff Springs Hotel and the Sanitarium with water from the Upper Hot Springs. He explained to the foreman that the vertical drop of 600 feet would create pressures of 250 pounds per square inch.

"Oh, I'm sure this here yoke will take the strain just foine, Sor."

"My good man," said Stewart, "you are absolutely wrong. That 'yoke,' as you put it, will soon turn into a sieve. However, don't tell me later that you weren't warned."

And the Superintendent reined his horse around and rode off, leaving the man to his business. The Banff Springs plumbers had chosen not to heed his advice either. There would be some tremendous geysers in the fine hotel when they turned the main valves on! The thought of it made him chuckle to himself. He could imagine Van Horne's outraged expression already. The chuckle brought a disapproving frown from a leading lady of the town, who was out collecting funds to build Banff's first church. He doffed his cap. "Morning, madame," he said pleasantly.

"Hmmph," she sniffed. Which reminded him; the whiskey pedlars were lurking about the station bush again. Connor would have to get down there and put a stop to that business. It was no good waiting for the Mounted Police to arrive. We can't have a bunch of drunken navvies terrorizing the tourists. Or was the lady miffed about the *Hot Springs Gazette* episode, he wondered. Most of the town had bought a year's subscription to the paper, which was to be published in Winnipeg. After one issue, the editor had absconded with the funds. Connor would have to write the Winnipeg police again.

What a nuisance; there was so much to do. Both the road to Lake Minnewanka (then called Devil's Lake) and the one to the Bow Falls viewpoint were slowed by the rains. There was talk of putting a steam launch on the Bow River and one at Lake Minnewanka. That meant piers, which of course everyone expected him to supply from the public purse. The folk were starting to mutter about the need for a firehouse. They had yet to put up much that burning could harm. And the rain; well, at least there wouldn't be any forest fires for a while. But I must get the men cutting fire guards around the town or, by jingo, one fine day the whole lot *will* burn down. Ah, here we are at the Cave. Quite an improvement from last year, but I wish the bathhouses were ready.

"Whoa, there."

All in all, it was a very busy programme for one man to carry out, as Head Surveyor, Town Planner, Chief of Public Works, de facto Mayor, Park Superintendent, Head Engineer, Chief of Police, and Head Magistrate. A man who also, incidentally, had yet to be informed (until August 1887) of the new name of the

Steam launch on the Bow River, ca.1890.

park he was running, or receive a copy of the act by which he was to regulate it. No wonder that Stewart made mistakes, and sometimes seemed abrupt and arbitrary in his decisions. A garbled telegram he received that summer ultimately led to his undoing. It should have read ''lots in park to be leased, not sold,'' but instead came out as ''leased, or sold.'' Stewart sold a number of lots before the error was realized, then had to compensate the buyers for their improvements and buy back the lots. This mistake would be remembered when the Liberal Party came to power in 1896.

Since the hot springs were the raison d'etre of the first national park, Stewart took special pains for their development, especially at the Cave and Basin, where the first government bathhouses were erected that summer. Built after the Swiss style and set on stone foundations, the two bathhouses were an immediate hit with the bathers. Visitors were kept at bay until that autumn, however, after a section of cliff collapsed into the Basin pool. The workmen escaped injury but, in the process of clearing rocks and deepening the pool, they discovered pockets of quicksand and some cold rills of water entering the warm pools. Stewart decided to enclose the pools with cement, and to install control valves to help regulate the temperature.

Stewart's efforts were done with economy, but the politicians in Ottawa raised their eyebrows at the price tag of all this ''improving.'' In six years it came to exactly $141,254.00 for the whole park. The resort attracted three thousand visitors in '87, a fact which Stewart wisely pointed out in his reports. But at ten cents per dip in the Cave and Basin, it would take a long time to ''recoup the Treasury.'' The numbers increased to five thousand in 1888, after the well publicized opening of the Banff Springs Hotel. And they would swell and swell every year after that, forcing the Banff Springs Hotel to turn away five thousand visitors in 1902, and clone itself into two wings by 1903 with double the occupancy. Long before then, the satisfied noises emanating from the Canadian Pacific Railway directors and Banff businessmen almost convinced the government that their expensive asset was worth the price.

The early success of its first reserve made the government receptive to the ideas advanced by William Pearce, and by the ubiquitous Van Horne, to reserve other beauty spots for park purposes. William Pearce, who had travelled the whole mountain route of the CPR in 1884, mostly on foot, was instrumental in setting aside reserves at Field, British Columbia, and at Mount Sir Donald and Rogers Pass. These forerunners of Yoho and Glacier national parks were set aside by an Order-in-Council of October 1886.

In 1892, a reserve of 132 square kilometres was set up in Lake Louise, where the CPR had built the first chalet in 1890. Lake Louise would be added to Rocky

Mountains National Park in 1902. Once again, the CPR had been instrumental in identifying park terrain that might otherwise have been assigned totally to logging or mining use. The company built carriage roads in the reserves where they had built their famous railroad hotels.

In practical terms, the other reserves could be described as CPR national parks, since for many years the government left their development in the hands of the CPR. For the next twenty-five years, the CPR supplied the only means of transportation into the parks, and was the leading hotelier in the Rockies. The government could exercise itself in parliament on the national parks as the "pleasure ground of the people," but the CPR was more interested in the class of people who could afford to pay the princely sum of $3.50 per diem at its hotels. It was the wealthy classes that patronized the great spas of Europe, and the company directed its advertising through newspapers, brochures, posters, and travelling displays at them. They were promised all the excitement of the wild west, without the pesky discomforts of hunger, restless natives, rough rides, and sudden death which had plagued the previous generation of travellers.

"You shall see mighty rivers," they were promised, "vast forests, boundless plains, stupendous mountains and wonders innumerable; and you shall see all in comfort, nay, in luxury."

The first Banff Springs Hotel, styled after the chateaux of the Loire, dominated the local hostelries in altitude, number of storeys, scenic situation, interior elegance, and cuisine. To make sure that newcomers knew which hotel to pick, the CPR's high-seated Tallyho, rising imperiously above the other hacks, had the best spot at the station exit.

As the Duke said to the Prince (according to one ad), "How high we live . . . .on the Canadian Pacific Railway." A more homely visitor to the Banff Springs commented on the height of the building, and said, "The only thing higher . . . .is the price of the drinks." But most visitors were suitably impressed with the Banff Springs, and by 1894 it was listed by *Baedeker's Guide* as one of the top hotels in the Dominion.

But the railroad, which had made the creation of the park possible in 1885, continued to plague it with the threat of fiery destruction for many years thereafter. In 1889 dense clouds of smoke covered the mountains and prairie from Vancouver to Medicine Hat. The Superintendent of Forestry attributed the forest fires "almost entirely (to) sparks from locomotives. On each side of the railroad track," he reported, "is a belt of felled timber which, on account of its extreme dryness, ignites easily and acts as a medium or train for conveying the fire to the forest. My reports from (British Columbia) estimate the loss . . . .at over $1,000,000.00. This could have been avoided had the smoke pipes of the engine been properly screened."

First Post Office 1886-87.

The first Banff Springs Hotel.

Sanitarium tally-ho.

Group of bathers after a dip.

A Garden In the Wilderness 71

The fires of 1889 not only befogged the scenery, but threatened to burn down the whole park, Banff Springs Hotel and all. While the guests coughed over their vintage wines and hacked in their teacups, extensive fires were seen approaching from the northwest. Stewart watched helplessly:

> No human efforts could avail to arrest the flames, but the bare summits of the mountains, which form a boundary, were effectual in arresting their progress. All that could be done . . . was to watch carefully for the sparks and masses of burning wood carried by the wind over the mountain and peaks and falling thousands of feet from their source. All the men on the works had to fight this demon, and the inhabitants were warned out to assist for days in cutting out fire breaks and preventing the spread of these fires down into the valleys of the park. The fires this season have been the most destructive known for many years and now that they are over it is satisfactory to know, that as regards the track of the fire . . . we can hardly be visited from the same quarter for some time to come.

Stewart returned uneasily to his task of developing the park, with the smell of woodsmoke constantly in his nostrils. Ravished nature had intruded itself unpleasantly into the nation's ''mountain playgrounds.''

There were requests from the CPR to extend the bridle paths in the townsite vicinity, and complaints from visitors about the ugliness of the townsite and the Cave and Basin. They expected, not unreasonably, the sort of pretty amenities usually associated with a park or zoological gardens: trees, flowers, and animals.

Stewart started a tree nursery with 40,000 imported specimens recommended by the Government Experimental Farm near Ottawa. The exotic trees shrivelled in the mountain climate, but the Superintendent had better luck in transplanting native trees on Banff Avenue and along the Bow River.

The ugly little frontier village of 1887 had changed over the years into a rustic mountain town with some of the niceties of a genteel resort settlement. One disgruntled travel writer complained that the town, though it had only one street, was ''horribly civilized.'' Visiting cowhands on a tear were certainly nonplussed by one of the regulations in the Park Act passed in 1890: ''Furious riding or driving on public roads . . . is prohibited,'' and furthermore, ''horses driven with sleighs shall be provided with bells.'' The North West Mounted Police were in residence to arrest angered equestrians and make sure all horses jingled while be-sledded.

On Sundays, the mountains echoed with church bells of four different denominations. There was a school for the education of the young, and a cemetery for the departed.

Burgeoning commerce in 1894.

There were also ten licensed liquor outlets to quench the thirst of the drinking population, estimated at about 250. The temperance movement had made serious inroads on the rest of the inhabitants. No saloons were allowed in Banff, under the Rocky Mountains Act, and no liquor was allowed to be served at local hotels on the Sabbath. But the liquor licenses were issued in Regina, and the inspector seldom visited the park. The retail outlets hit on some happy compromises to get around the liquor laws, which soon had the local Good Templars Society up in arms. The parsons of Banff directed most of their invective at a certain house in the nearby mining town of Anthracite (founded in 1886), where the fires of thirst and lust could be assuaged simultaneously.

One of the tipplers who scandalously toppled out of a so-called drugstore into the glaring daylight of Banff Avenue was none other than Inspector Harper of the Banff NWMP. Some of his constables were often seen frequenting Dr. Brett's Sanitarium, where the good doctor was apparently prescribing medicine beyond the legally appointed hours. His Sunday services were the answer to an alcoholic's prayers. Stewart sent a scathing indictment of Inspector Harper's abilities to the Minister of the Interior.

The strident campaign against the boozers in Banff and Anthracite, led by Superintendent Stewart, raised hackles in the park and eyebrows in Ottawa. Some of the Banff citizens that Stewart criticized in his reports had been nursing grudges over his handling of leases in the park since 1887, and their complaints were noted by the Liberal government that came to power in 1896.

Clifford Sifton was not pleased with the Department of the Interior that he took over in November of that year. According to his biographer, John W. Defoe, the Minister felt that "it was a department of delay, a department of circumlocution . . . which tired men to death who undertook to get any business transacted with it." Sifton made a number of changes, and his new Deputy Minister, James A. Smart, felt that George Stewart must go in favour of a "younger man, it being considered that the latter would be in a better position to . . . remove the grievances complained of."

For ten years, with little direction from Ottawa to guide his decisions, Stewart had worked hard to "make a park"; a civilized garden in a wilderness, for such was the view of parks in his time. Sandwiched between the citizens and the government, given little direction except to make the park useful as soon as possible, Stewart was ultimately made the scapegoat for the government's lack of park policy. Politics, too, played a part in his undoing. Few government jobs, no matter how lowly, could be held on the basis of ability alone in those days. Party meant a lot and the Liberals had just replaced the Conservatives. Stewart was also a blunt and sometimes undiplomatic man, which did not help his career.

He left his stamp on the roads and streets of Banff, and on the Cave and Basin. His name is remembered today by Stewart Canyon, where the Cascade River empties into the manmade reservoir of today's Lake Minnewanka. It seems an appropriate, if ironic, salute to a parksman who was essentially a shaper of nature's landscapes, and a builder of bridges, buildings, and roadways.

Original North West Mounted Police barracks, ca.1890.

Dr. Brett's Drug Store, 1893.

The Sanitarium, ca. 1890, where "the good doctor was apparently prescribing 'medicine' beyond the legally appointed hours."

Howard Douglas, second Superintendent, who helped bring the buffalo back to the Canadian Plains.

*I*n the days when a park vehicle license cost two dollars for the season, the gate keeper would issue you a small bronze buffalo to wire to the grill of your automobile. That was the park permit; a reminder of the work of Howard Douglas, who helped bring the buffalo back to the Canadian plains.

It falls to some men, who enter public office in a time of transition, to spend their whole careers revising their ideas; they are caught in the conflicting winds of change. Such was the case of the second superintendent of Rocky Mountains National Park.

Douglas had worked for the Canadian Pacific Railway and was a coal merchant in Calgary when the wheel of political fortune set him in a new role as park superintendent. Though the Grits had swept the Tories out of office, at least one notion of Sir John A.'s was merely dusted off and polished up to serve the new regime. "Recoup the Treasury" was what he'd promised the first national park would do for the government. The phrase was to haunt park superintendents for many years. Douglas, a commercially-minded man, would operate the park with one eye on his budget throughout his career. But the other eye, tied to an inquiring mind, peered into the future, poring over the philosophies of the day.

Perhaps our generation has lost that peculiar aesthetic sense familiar to our great-grandfathers: that particular rapture they experienced at the sight of slag heaps and belching smokestacks; the pleasure they took in seeing new buildings, no matter how ugly, rising in the heart of virgin wilderness. The buildings and the factories and mines were perhaps as rare to them then, and as needed for peace of mind, as a vista unmarred by powerlines is to us now. Only reluctantly would the frontiersmen admit that their insatiable lusting after raw materials could not go on indefinitely.

One man whose ideas flew in the face of this predatory civilization was John Muir, an American author, mountaineer and "preservationist." Muir, like the transcendentalist writers Thoreau and Emerson, refused to apply the dollar standard to wilderness land. Wilderness to him was precious, priceless by its very existence. He maintained that over-civilized people needed the spiritual solace to be found only in the wilderness, the "fountain of life," as he called it. He was a great forerunner of the environmentalists and conservationists of today.

In Rocky Mountains Park, the practical-minded Douglas was exposed for the first time to John Muir's disciples, the elegant tourist-mountaineers who had come to climb the virgin peaks of the Canadian Rockies.

The first tourists to the Banff Park area were admiring the scenery and harassing the railroad construction crews with questions a year before the park reserve was set aside. A railroad engineer, Collingwood Schreiber, wrote a prophetic comment on the Bow Valley to the Minister of Railways in 1884: "If I mistake it not, it will be a great resort for tourists and madmen who like climbing mountains at the risk of breaking their necks."

The prospect of climbing virgin peaks in unknown territory proved a powerful drawing card to climbers and adventurers from the U.S. and Europe. When they arrived in the Rockies, they found very few people who could tell them about climbing conditions here. One man who could have given advice (if you could find him) was the surveyor, J. J. McArthur, who climbed mountains routinely as part of his work on the topographical survey of the Rocky Mountains.

Guides Edward Feuz and Rudolph Aemmer with ladies of the Alpine Club of Canada camp on Storm Mountain.

A Grand and Fabulous Notion

"Lunching 5,000 feet in the air," he reported laconically in 1887, "seated on the edge of a snowbank with a ham sandwich in one hand and a snowball in the other, is about as poor comfort as anyone could wish for." He compared the Rockies to the teeth of a saw turned upwards. Through the forested gaps of the sawteeth, he and his men chopped their way with axes. They ascended the peaks to take photographs and set survey signals, climbing with heavy box cameras and surveying equipment on their backs.

A typical entry in his reports reads, "We took five hours to make the ascent of 3,300 feet from camp, sometimes ploughing our way along steep slopes where a snow slide might sweep us into eternity, or crawling on hands and knees across deep ravines drifted full of snow." For a number of years, McArthur was the sole authority on climbing routes in the Canadian Rockies, but he was often in the field and hard to consult for directions.

So the tourists found themselves cast in the role of explorers and pioneers. They came equipped with tricuni-nailed boots, manila ropes, cameras, and sometimes their own surveying instruments. They climbed the unknown peaks, and "discovered" passes and lakes that had been previously known only to Indians, or had been found and forgotten by white fur traders many years before. These genteel adventurers often had scientific or literary interests. Some of them produced popular books on their travels. Others published maps, or reports on the flora and fauna. Their efforts were actively encouraged by the CPR because such publications had good effect in arousing the public's interest in the Rockies and increasing the tourist trade among the wealthy classes.

Douglas too was pleased by the maps and articles published by the tourist explorers of the '90s. The publicity helped to sustain visitation during a time of recession, and he could point out with pride that his park drew twice as many visitors as the famous Yellowstone did from 1890 to 1895. These visitors were not all mountaineers. They included wealthy trophy hunters who had heard of the remaining stocks of black bear, grizzly, sheep and goats said to dwell in the valleys outside the national park. (In those pioneer days, many of the alpinists also came equipped with rifles, to collect specimens or just to shoot game for the pot.)

In 1887, when a group of hunters arrived at the springs looking for sport beyond the main valley, there was no one to act as an outfitter and guide. The CPR turned to Tom Wilson, who had been a faithful servant to Major Rogers on the railroad survey. Wilson was then working for the railroad building a trail into Lake Louise. Wilson had been the first white man to see Lake Louise. He had been guided there in 1882 by a Stoney named Gold Seeker. This same Indian took the first prospector to the copper diggings near Castle Mountain (later known as Silver City).

Above: Plain of 6 Glaciers, 1903.

Opposite: Victoria Glacier (upper left).
Paradise Valley (lower left).
Ptarmigan Valley (right).

Above: Tom Wilson, outfitter, guide and trailblazer, the first white man to see Lake Louise.

Opposite: The legendary "Wild" Bill Peyto (upper right).
Excerpt from Banff Crag and Canyon, *Oct. 25, 1913 (lower right).*
Tom Wilson and Morley Beaver on Kootenay Plains, 1900 (left).

Outside of the trails at Banff and Lake Louise, radiating out for a few kilometres from the Bow Valley, there were no pleasant, graded routes into the back country as we find them today: only the game trails and paths left by the Indians and the white traders that had followed in their wake. Wilson's vehicle of discovery was the same one that had opened up the West and carried the traders and surveyors after them: the Indian cayuse. Wilson had started an outfitting business in Banff, and the packers and guides who worked for him were a wild-eyed bunch, eccentrics to a man.

Most singular of all was "Wild" Bill Peyto, a transplanted Englishman whose native eccentricities took root and flowered to excess in the stony earth of the Rockies. Peyto stories are part of the folklore of Banff. My favourite is one told by guide Tex Woods. He pulled into one of Peyto's cabins one time, and was just boiling the tea kettle, when the door flew open and a grizzly bear charged into the cabin with an enraged bellow. Tex was terrified. But it was only Wild Bill, wrapped in the raw and bleeding hide of a bear he had just killed.

The wealthy men who travelled with these guides published many lively accounts of their travels in the sporting and mountaineering magazines. The CPR was naturally pleased with Wilson's business and the publicity he created. But the colourful guides and their wealthy hunters, first welcomed by Superintendent Douglas, eventually began to make him nervous. The more educated classes had begun to lament the near extinction of the great buffalo herds, and there was a growing interest in the fate of the wild animals that remained. Douglas was deeply impressed by the effect the park wildlife had on his visitors. Any stray bighorn ram or black bear that wandered into sight was immediately surrounded by crowds of enthralled sightseers. Here was a valuable resource, reasoned the practical Douglas, that people wanted to see. Yet game was rarely seen in the Bow Valley. What the public usually saw were the hides and heads of animals packed into Banff by the guides and their wealthy clients. It was also obvious to Douglas that many hunting trophies were being taken inside the park boundaries. Hunting in the park had not been prohibited by regulation until 1890, and Douglas, like his predecessor Stewart, longed for a staff of game wardens. "I find great difficulty in enforcing the laws . . . as game is generally killed in the more remote districts, and offenders are careful to see that their actions are unobserved. There is great difficulty in securing evidence."

Douglas mounted a campaign to hire full-time game wardens to control the illegal hunting. Although he had some seasonally employed wardens, he didn't trust them. "They are inclined to wink at breaches of the law," he complained, "rather than incur the enmity of their neighbours." It would be another thirteen years before the first permanent man was hired. In the meantime, Douglas relied on

Wanted to See a Bear

A small group of tourists including a British army officer, at Field early this wesk, expressed a burning desire to see "a live b'ar" in his native haunts.. So Jack Giddy hooked up a team and toted the party out towards Emerald lake. Meeting a slide in the road they left the rig and ran plumb into a grizzly. The bear arose on his haunches, when Jack pumped a bullet into him, and then charged the party. A couple more well-aimed shots put bruin out of commission. The tourists expressed their perfect satisfaction.

the North West Mounted Police to secure occasional convictions against poachers. But there were as yet no effective game laws to regulate hunting in the North West Territories. The prohibition against hunting in the park was therefore a novelty that many hunters did not take seriously.

Nevertheless, Douglas decided that the park must be enlarged to bring all big game habitat and scenic attractions under government control; the same request had been made by George Stewart in 1894, to no avail. Douglas' request found popular support in the western newspapers, the predominant opinion being that parks were good for business. He argued that with the creation of the western provinces now imminent, lands should be set aside at once to avoid problems with the new authority. His arguments were seconded by William Pearce, always a friend of the park idea, who continued to keep an eye on park developments throughout his career.

Douglas, an aggressive businessman before he was a civil servant, took steps to increase the game population while the Minister was making up his mind about expansion. He decided to build a paddock where game could be observed by the visitors, and protected under his watchful eye. The first specimens of this enclosure were a small herd of elk, soon followed by two buffalo cows purchased in Texas

Above: Trail guide Tom Lusk was possibly from the Lone Star State, since he had come across the border "with a Texas sheriff in hot pursuit." Tom's true avocation was drinking whiskey. He had a ranch near Cochrane and the outhouse, built of empty whiskey boxes, was the monument to his prowess. He was also one of the best horsemen around, and became Wilson's head guide.

Right: Jim Brewster and friend with grizzly skin.

by T. G. Blackstock, Q.C., of Toronto, and donated to the park.   Douglas enlarged the paddock to 200 hectares when Lord Strathcona donated thirteen more buffalo from his private herd in Manitoba. There were additions of mountain lions, red foxes, and mountain sheep. The whole menagerie was ruled by Sir Donald, the largest buffalo in North America. Captured near Fort Garry in 1872, he ruled supreme at the paddock until his death in 1908, when some younger bulls gored the senile monarch to death. By that time, many of the animals had been moved into Banff, where a zoo was opened near the present government museum in 1907.

The idea of a zoo in a national park, with iron bars and wire fences, would cause any modern conservationist to immediately reach for her hacksaw and bolt cutters. But Douglas' ''experiment,'' as it was described at the time, was pivotal in

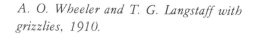

A. O. Wheeler and T. G. Langstaff with grizzlies, 1910.

Above: Mountain goat in paddock.

Right: "Moose Billy" with Ben Woodworth, caretaker at Banff Animal Paddock, 1916.

changing the attitudes on wildlife preservation in the national parks. For the first time, the government looked at its stock of wild animals as a resource that had a value beyond the price of fur: they were seen as an asset, and a potentially valuable one, as a source of interest to tourists.

The Honourable Clifford Sifton decided in favour of his Superintendent's request, and in 1902 Parliament passed an amendment to the Rocky Mountains Park Act, which increased its size to 1,780 hectares. The park now included the Lake Louise reserve, the beautiful Kananaskis Lakes on the eastern edge of the mountains, as well as the watersheds of the Red Deer and Spray rivers.

Douglas, not content to rest on this fine achievement, continued to press for an effective warden service for the park. At the same time, he searched far and wide for more specimens for his paddock. In 1901 he hired one William Margach of Rat Portage, Ontario, to seduce four Ontario moose into emigrating west to Alberta. In doing so, he raised the ire of the Chief Warden of the Ontario Game Commission. This official wrote to Margach in 1904: "Dear Sir: I have your letter of March 7th, enclosing one from Mr. Stewart Douglas (sic) . . . in which he offers several hundred dollars to induce you to again violate the Ontario Game Protection Act." The irate warden threatened to prosecute Margach for illegally exporting game, and added, "I am sending a copy of Mr. Douglas' letter to the

Hon. Minister of the Interior, with such comments as Mr. Douglas' conduct deserves.''

This setback had little effect on the irrepressible moose rustler, Howard Douglas. He was determined to undo the damage that the railroad and the un-policed hunters had done to ''his'' park, and restock both fish and mammals as quickly as possible. Douglas' thinking on conservation was evolving and showing some of the confusion that great but undigested ideas can create in aspiring minds. In his annual report for 1902, he told his minister, ''All the mountains are still rich in wildness and by means of good roads are being brought nearer civilization every year; the wildest health and pleasure grounds are made accessible and available to many a lover of wildness who without them would never see it.'' The state-ment is a direct quote from Muir's writings, as Janet Foster has pointed out in her book *Working for Wildlife.* Muir and Douglas would turn over in their graves if they could see what highways have done to today's North American wilderness.

Douglas' reputation as a procurer of wild critters resulted in a chance to go after much bigger game: the biggest herd of buffalo then remaining in North America. They were owned by Michel Pablo, a Spanish-speaking rancher whose grazing privileges on the Flathead Reservation in Montana were to be rescinded in 1905. Pablo went to Washington and offered to sell his herd to the govern-ment. President Roosevelt favoured the purchase, but Congress refused to pass the appropriation. The embittered Pablo approached the Canadian authorities several times before Douglas was finally dispatched to size up the herd.

Douglas and Pablo took a liking to each other immediately. The seventy-year-old Pablo was a *''mucho mucho hombre,''* a natural leader of cowboys, who led from the saddle. Douglas was determined to buy the herd which Pablo estimated at 350 animals, and for which he wanted two hundred dollars a head. But the Canadian government dragged its feet while Douglas harangued his superiors on the need to move fast. The herd was within one hundred kilometres of Yellowstone National Park, and Douglas feared interference from that quarter if the deal was not concluded quickly. The crafty Superintendent finally appealed to patriotism to close the deal. He sent Deputy-Minister William Cory a news clipping dated January 17. It reported on the plans of the American Bison Society to buy up all private buffalo herds in the U.S. The new Minister, the Hon. Frank Oliver, showed it to the Prime Minister, and soon Douglas received a telegram ordering him to close the deal.

As it turned out, it would take Pablo from 1907 to 1912 to round up all the buffalo, using twenty to thirty of the best cowboys he could find. Unlike domestic cattle, buffalo made a routine practise of turning and charging their assailants en

''Howard Douglas was determined to restock the depleted supplies of fish and wildlife.''

Michel Pablo and wife. "A natural leader of cowboys, who led from the saddle."

masse. The first old bull to be herded into a boxcar simply continued right on through the far wall, causing one onlooker to cry gleefully, "Hey Pablo, is them what you call the vanishing buffalo?"

Ranging the hills, Pablo's men kept finding more and more buffalo, and Douglas urged his Minister to buy every one Pablo could find. The politicians seemed to close ranks on the buffalo issue and voted the appropriations without much argument. "Out-Yanking the Yankees," as one Montana paper put it, and jerking the buffalo out from under American noses, had become a source of national pride. In the end, the herd totalled 703. The buffalo came home again to Buffalo National Park, founded in August 1907 near Wainwright, Alberta, where there were remains of old buffalo wallows and the bones of the once countless beasts. Others were held at Elk Island Park east of Edmonton. This small park of forty-two square kilometres had been set aside in 1904, inspired by the Rocky Mountains Park example, to preserve a threatened herd of elk from destruction by hunters.

By 1907, Douglas' passion for wildlife seems to have led him far down the wilderness path of John Muir. This former coal merchant had once described the coal mining town of Bankhead (established in 1904) as a "handsome modern town" and an "attraction" to the park visitor. But in 1907, he told the Minister of the Interior that no further mining or timber leases should be allowed in the park. "Large camps of men . . . lead to every possible breach of the laws for the protection of the game." Now his reports contained no encomiums to industry, but tributes to "the beautiful yellow erythranium pushing through the spring snow," and to the "crimson calypso, the prettiest orchid on earth."

Howard Douglas' greatest contribution to the National Parks movement was in the long hoped-for creation of the park Fire and Game Guardian Service (later known as the Warden Service) in 1909. The National Park General Regulations enabled the Minister to appoint "game guardians" with sweeping police powers to control illegal hunting and lighting of open fires. The regulations contained many of the recommendations Douglas had made to provide for the sealing of firearms in the park, the control of dogs that harassed game, establishing seasons for sport fishing, and outlawing netting and dynamiting of fish.

The first warden contingent was pathetically small for the patrolling of forty-two square kilometres. It consisted of three cowboys wearing tin badges and tall Stetsons. But Douglas had appointed a Chief Fire and Game Warden well equipped to set up the new force and to develop guidelines for its operation. Howard E. Sibbald had lived and travelled in the foothills and mountains for thirty years. For the first time, the park superintendent had a means of enforcing regulations throughout the park. The long arm of Sibbald's law stretched far into the Red

Deer River country and collared several poachers in 1910, with salutary effect on the local hunters. If they still boasted about poaching, they now did it in whispers, while looking over their shoulders.

By 1913, moose began to drift back into the Bow Valley; by 1914, deer were commonly seen on the town avenues and wild sheep were posing for pictures west of town. The new Superintendent reported, ''I am firmly convinced that the sense of the wild animals in the park had told them that they are protected . . . all game is now less timid of the approach of man.''

The zoo that Douglas created survived until 1937, when the department decided it was no longer an appropriate feature in the park and closed it down. A small herd of buffalo still ranged the paddock near Banff in 1984, as a poignant reminder of how close the mighty herds once came to extinction. The buffalo, and the herds of deer and bighorn sheep that now throng the Bow Valley, are a part of the legacy left to posterity by Howard Douglas. He came to Rocky Mountains Park as a political appointee and merchant, and left it as a great preserver of wildlife and landscape. Fortune's wheel had chosen well.

The Pablo buffalo roundup. Howard Douglas is second from left.

A Grand and Fabulous Notion

*I*n July of 1911, the Twentieth Century, in the shape of America's great democratizing vehicle of change, the Model T Ford, crashed the gates of Banff's private reserve for the wealthy. "The doubtful class," as Sir John A. had once described the ordinary man, had arrived at last and was here to stay. The next great transformation of Rocky Mountains Park was underway.

That same year, the new Minister of the Interior, the Hon. Frank Oliver, had created the Dominion Parks Branch. Enacted under the Dominion Forest Reserves and Parks Act, the world's first national park bureau consolidated the parks under one administration. Along with the first national park, the reserves at Yoho, Glacier, Jasper and Waterton were now to be known as "Dominion Parks." The buffalo sanctuary at Wainwright and the Elk Island reserve were part of the Branch. Although the Parks Branch would come under a number of different departments over the years, it would always maintain a separate identity and a special sense of purpose and idealism; much of the credit for that goes to the Branch's first Commissioner, J. B. Harkin.

The appointment in June 1911 was notably inauspicious. James B. Harkin was private secretary to Oliver at the time. He was thirty-six, and a former newspaper editor who had changed careers to become "political secretary" to Clifford Sifton

Opposite: Caretaker David D. Galletly and friend at Basin, ca.1900.

Left: Old Bow Bridge. "The twentieth century, in the shape of the Model T Ford, crashed the gates of Banff."

J. B. (Bunny) Harkin, appointed first Dominion Parks Branch Commissioner in 1911. Under his leadership the number of parks was tripled to eighteen by 1932.

in 1901. The first Commissioner, known as "Bunny" to his close friends, was a mild-mannered man for such a prominent position. He was an enlightened thinker, and a wide-ranging reader in the field of conservation. He was also a devout Christian who came to see the wilderness as the ultimate expression of God's handiwork. His efforts on behalf of the National Parks movement were in the nature of a personal crusade. He was honest and modest.

"I know nothing about parks!" he told Oliver on the day of his promotion.

The Minister smiled at his discomfiture. "All the better," he said in his laconic way. "You won't be hampered by preconceived ideas and you can find out."

Harkin took the plunge, and fell immediately into hot water. By the Act mentioned above, the parks were placed in a dominion forest preserve that took in some 64,000 square kilometres. A clause in the Act, apparently put in to satisfy the mining and lumbering interests of the day, provided for the lease of suitable lands "for trade and industry" by Order-in-Council. Using the excuse that the vast areas of park lands could not be administered or protected by the small staff available, the government began reducing the size of the national parks. Rocky Mountains was cut to 4,700 square kilometres, Jasper shrank from 13,000 down to 2,600 square kilometres: even tiny Waterton Park was reduced in size.

The little ship of the embryo Parks Branch was sent reeling under a storm of protest. The Campfire Club of America and the Alberta Fish and Game Protective Association were upset about the effect on game preservation. The Canadian Northern and Grand Truck Pacific railways, fully committed to promoting Jasper Park as a tourist destination, got their steam up and demanded an immediate return of the former park boundaries. Howard Douglas, now Chief Superintendent and based in Edmonton, also urged the Minister not to reduce Rocky Mountains Park. He described the action as a "suicidal policy" as far as game protection was concerned.

After studying the boundaries and the reports on game breeding areas, Commissioner Harkin made the restoration of the old boundaries one of his priorities. Although his main concern was the protection of game, he used the commercial value of the parks to tourism to convince the Minister of the need for expansion. By 1914, Jasper was enlarged to 10,400 square km; by 1917, as a result negotiations between rival department heads, Harkin convinced his Minister to press for enlargement of Rocky Mountains Park to just over 7,000 square km.

This initiation under fire was perhaps the best training the new Commissioner could have. His motto became: "What we have, we hold." Looking at the timber berths and mining operations in the national parks, he saw that merely setting aside parks was no guarantee of their sanctity. For the next nineteen years he worked to create a separate National Parks Act which would protect the parks from all future industrial exploitation.

In the fall of 1911, the Commissioner headed west to inspect his new charges. He was deeply impressed with the beauty of the mountain parks, and greatly perturbed at the thousands of dollars in appropriations needed for improvements, especially for motor roads.

When it came to the use of automobiles in Rocky Mountains Park, the government, urged on by the livery operators, had tried to stop the clock. After the first automobile nosed into town in 1904, mounted with flanged wheels to ride the railroad, the government reacted by banning all automobiles from the park. In 1909, an auto driven by Norman Lougheed wheezed triumphantly up Banff Avenue and was promptly impounded by the North West Mounted Police.

By 1913, North America's love affair with the passenger car was in full swing. Fifty thousand tin lizzies were clattering into every corner of the Dominion. The national parks were behind the times (or rather, ahead of the times, some would argue today). The motorists were clamouring for improved roads in the mountains. A provincial road was under construction to the park boundary, and in 1911, the Calgary Auto Club had roared defiantly into town, pursued despairingly by the NWMP, to the consternation of all lovers of horseflesh.

"Despite the best of intentions the automobile became a fact of life in the park."

Until 1916 cars would have to be ''checked'' at the police barracks in Banff, and the motorists dismounted. There were few roads suitable for motorists anyway, but there was tremendous agitation for improvement and new construction. The thinly-gravelled streets of Banff, dotted with horse dung and noisome with flies in sunny weather, turned into mud wallows in the rain. Money would have to be found for roadwork; the park was booming and the dust was flying in the wake of the carriages and tallyhos.

As Harkin toured the town with his officials, he found the hot springs were rivalled only by the zoo and the park buffalo herd as the main attractions. Banff's entrepreneurs were still intoxicated by the smell of sulphur. One hotelier used the government-owned waters not only for his bathing business, but for cooking, drinking, and ''steaming his carriages.'' The Commissioner, a frugal man, decided to charge him more money for the privilege.

The good Doctor Brett, perhaps inspired by his previous encounter with the temperance movement, had discovered the soft drink market. Brett established the Sanitarium Bottling Company to convert the sulphur water into a palatable drink, advertised as ''Banff Lithia Water.'' This bathtub gin for teetotallers was aimed at the health seekers who previously had to sip drinking water from the Cave spring from an enamelled cup hanging from a chain on the wall.

Above: Banff Springs Hotel and Bow Falls. View from Tunnel Mtn., ca.1920.

Right: Mount Stephen Hall, Banff Springs Hotel.

The Banff Springs Hotel was perhaps the biggest consumer of the sulphur water. Due to some of the plumbing problems that Stewart had predicted in 1887, the first Banff Springs could not always obtain enough water for their plunges. The staff solved the problem by surreptitiously adding hot water early in the morning, then throwing in bags of sulphur mineral and stirring the brew with a paddle. By 1911, the Hotel had solved its plumbing problems, but it was crazily overbooked and turning people away in droves. The CPR began work that fall on a series of additions that would culminate in today's hotel, the beautiful castle by Bow Falls, completed in 1928. By 1912, the Hotel offered sulphur or fresh water swimming in two separate pools. Guests could also elect to sweat their way through ''Russian'' and ''Turkish'' baths, be pounded asleep by a masseur, and revived by a cold plunge or shower. It was truly an oasis of the ostentatious.

The government's bathing facilities paled by comparison. At the Upper Hot Springs, a modest but relatively new structure was put up by the crafty Douglas after two private bathhouses conveniently burned down. Although Douglas had

built a new pool at the Basin in 1903, there was standing room only when Harkin visited, and the bathhouses, extended in 1903-04, were already inadequate.

The whole operation had become as quaint and outmoded as the sign on the wall that read: ''It is compulsory for all to wear costumes.'' The style of the lower springs was set by its elderly Scots caretaker and guide, David D. Galletly. Coal oil lamp in hand, this first and most outrageous of park naturalists would take visitors on a tour into the cave, through the low tunnel built in 1887. Fortunately, one of Galletly's spiels, delivered one Hallowe'en, was recorded by a writer of the *Nor'West Farmer Magazine*. Perhaps the Commissioner was favoured with a similar account during his autumn visit.

According to Galletly, the tunnel was not carved by George Stewart, but blasted out by a satanic flatulence in the nether world and the smell of rotten eggs in the cave drifted up from the infernal regions of hell.

As the lamplight played eerily over the cave pool, Galletly pointed out a bat-shaped rock where ''Mephistopheles'' would sit every Hallowe'en — and play the bagpipes.

It seems the Devil is the king of pipers. At the first skirl of the pipes, the Devil's imps left their task of running the infernal boilers that heated the hot springs, and came flying up through the ''geysers'' to dance the highland fling. Galletly, elevated by a bottle of ''Sanderson's Mountain Dew,'' danced with them, but refused to ''pay the piper.''

Left: Upper Hot Springs, ca.1912.

Above: Upper Hot Springs, ca.1906.

David D. Galletly, guide and caretaker at the Lower Springs. His imaginative tours made him a tourist attraction in his own right.

"Hey, Davie!" cried the arch fiend, "Hand me ower the bottle."

"Na, na, Auld Clooty," answered Galletly. "I remember the first nicht we celebrated here. I was gallant enough to gie ye the first drink an' ye deevil, ye drank it a' . . . .Skirl up yer pipes, ye auld rascal, on with the dance!"

Galletly's hydrology lecture was entertaining, though not particularly informative. The old caretaker was Harkin's secret weapon at the Cave and Basin, however, and many a tourist was drawn to the place just to make his acquaintance.

Harkin gave the needs of the Cave and Basin much of his attention on his return to Ottawa. In 1912 Walter Painter of Painter and Swales, Architects, was engaged to submit a design for a pool and bathhouse. Walter Painter had been chief architect to the CPR since 1905. He was busy at the time of Harkin's tour with designing new wings for both the Banff Springs Hotel and Chateau Lake Louise, and planning the new swimming pools at the Hotel. He would carry some aspects of the Banff Springs pool design into the Cave and Basin plans.

The Commissioner was pleased with Painter's design, but blanched at the $200,000 estimate. He sent it off to the Minister, however, urging a quick approval to get the building up for the next season.

The first excavation, beginning in the fall of 1912, was a contractor's nightmare. The main problem was the treacherous nature of the saturated tufa, or "semi-rock," as they called it back then. Some 1,300 cubic metres of this crud had to be removed from the site of the new bathhouse, which was designed as a hollow retaining structure to be dug into the mountainside. But in digging deeper for the foundation the men ran into lenses of quicksand, and the engineer had to abandon plans for a cement foundation. Instead, 300 twenty-centimetre-square fir piles were driven in in clusters to support some of the buttresses and part of the swimming pool. Teams of horses worked in the deepening snow to run two heavy pile drivers. On November 4, the Park Superintendent reported, "Bottom ends of piles at from 24 feet to 27 feet below datum. At this depth they move from two inches to four inches with a 20-foot drop of a 2,000-pound hammer."

All this horsing around was slow and expensive. The men were inclined to work in accord with the ancient motto of the park contractor: "Close enough for government work." Apparently, they were also a tad careless; while swotting away in the Public Archives one day, I found this enigmatic note from Harkin to Park Superintendent A. B. Macdonald: "Enquire immediately of man in hospital where dynamite hidden and have it stored suitably without delay."

At last, on January 1, 1913, the foundation work was complete. Now it was a case of "hurry up and wait," as contract arrangements and funding problems stopped progress on the superstructure. It was finally completed in December 1914.

The shape of the finished structure owes much to Painter's travels in Europe. According to his daughter, Mrs. Betty Walker of Banff, Painter had been sent abroad by the CPR to study the romantic chateaux of the Loire. Writing on Painter's design of the Banff Springs, Bart Robinson attributes Painter's work to the "Scottish Baronial tradition," itself inspired by the French chateaux. This is shown in the numerous arches that he used at the hotel swimming pool. At the Cave and Basin, the wide arch and gracious belvederes at the east end of the main pool were influenced by the building style of the Italian Tyrol, according to a friend of the architect's. Two more of these airy belvederes, roofed with red Spanish title, were to be located at the west end of the structure: one over the original basin pool, and one over a smaller pool. Regrettably, this gracious balance of forms never saw construction.

The central attraction was the swimming pool; at sixty-five metres long and eleven metres wide, it was the largest pool in the country at that time. It was protected from the north wind by a beautiful arcade wall, its six arches holding plate glass shields. The south wall of the structure rose in two tiers capped by a promenade deck. Behind the wall and under the decks were the changing rooms. The whole building was beautifully faced with Rundle rock from a quarry Painter had opened on the Spray River. Blue-grey when quarried, it changes to varying earthtones of brown with age. The sunlit building, with its red-roofed belvederes and red-tiled floors, had 200 square metres of translucent "Luxifer prism lights" (glass blocks), which formed the ceiling of the bathhouse and the floor of the promenade deck. Spectators could watch the swimmers and gaze out over the Bow Valley. With some of the flavour of an ancient Roman bath, it is a truly grand yet whimsical structure. Widely hailed as a masterpiece when erected, the Cave and Basin retains the feeling of a place built for unhurried enjoyment and celebration of life.

That was very important to the Commissioner. It was an aesthetically pleasing structure in accord with his own philosophy, as he once expressed it: "I feel that everything our engineers construct in the parks should be dominated by the spirit of beauty."

J. B. Harkin was very much a philosopher on national parks and often his statements bordered on the metaphysical. "People sometimes accuse me of being a mystic about the influences of the mountains," he once said. "Perhaps I am. I devoutly believe that there are emanations from them, intangible but very real, which elevate the mind and purify the spirit." This theme of the ennobling beneficent powers of nature was one he would return to again and again in his annual reports to the Minister, and in his addresses to sportsmen's clubs and other organizations interested in parks. "The further we have been from nature," he would tell them,

Walter Painter, architect of a masterpiece.

Right: The wide and gracious belvederes were influenced by the style of the Italian Tyrol.''

Below: ''The shape of the finished structure owes much to Painter's travels in Europe.''

Swim race at Banff Winter Carnival.

"the more we need to get back to the natural and even primitive life. Such a life allows man to resume his relationship with wild animals, a relationship as old as man himself and which every man takes pleasure in renewing."

"The day will come," he wrote prophetically, "when the population of Canada will be ten times as great as it is now, but the National Parks ensure that every Canadian, by right of citizenship, will still have free access to vast areas . . . .in which the beauty of the landscape is protected from profanation, the natural wild animals, plants, and forests preserved, and the peace and solitude of primeval nature retained."

Here was a man who had a very clear idea of what national parks were for, and not just for the present generation. The only legitimate purposes, as far as he was concerned, were the recreation of the public, scientific study, the education of the young by contact with nature, and the preservation of plant and animal life. Many of his ideas, including those quoted above, are contained in a booklet entitled *The Origin and Meaning of the National Parks of Canada.* Most of these ideas, formulated in the early years of his tenure, are as relevant to the parks of the future as they were to the parks of the past.

But this complex man, whose ideas on wilderness were far ahead of his time, had a streak of shrewdness and old-fashioned horse sense. Harkin's training in journalism had given him an eloquence and verbal polish that stood him well as a champion of parks, but his knowledge of the political animal, gained as secretary to the Minister of the Interior left him with few illusions about the aesthetic sense of most politicians. "How could the hard-headed members of the House of Commons be persuaded to increase parks' appropriations?" he asked himself in 1913.

He told them of his hopes and visions, of the noble purposes of parks, in every annual report. But he also told them that, "Nothing attracts tourists like national parks. National parks provide the chief means of bringing to Canada a stream of tourists and a stream of tourist gold." And he dragged forth travel statistics for the first time to prove his argument; statistics on tourist spending that he sent to every member of the House of Commons. When the Hon. Arthur Meighen (then Minister of the Interior) rose and defended park expenses, quoting from Harkin's figures, the vote of approval passed with little objection.

It was a method Harkin used time and time again to get the appropriations he needed. He even went so far (in 1915) as to compare the value in dollars of an acre of park land to an acre of wheat. The prairie farmer would not be surprised to learn that it was $13.88 to $4.91 — in favour of the mountain scenery, which is mainly composed of rock.

"What a revenue this country will obtain," he told the Minister in 1920, "when thousands of automobiles are traversing the parks." Harkin, like Steve Mather his American counterpart, did not at first see the tremendous damage that unrestricted number of automobiles would do, particularly to the park's wildlife. That would come with the high speed roads and heavy traffic of our own era.

Harkin was caught in the same vicious circle of development that his predecessors had tried to deal with. The parks must justify themselves by generating revenue, and like any business, increased patronage (tourism), comes from increased development (swimming pools and highways), which requires increased funding to be justified by increased visitation.

As his experience widened and as use of the parks increased, the Commissioner came to realize the central problem of all national parks:

"Use without abuse" — how can it be attained? . . . The parks belong to the people by right of citizenship . . . It is the duty of those in charge to make them freely accessible by road and trail, and to permit under regulation the provision of accommodation, refreshments, and other needs. But the more the parks are used, the more difficult it is to prevent abuse . . . The parks may lose the very thing that distinguished them from the outside world."

One abuse that Harkin had made up his mind to remove was industrial exploitation of park lands. After two decades of effort, he finally achieved that goal when

Boating on the Bow, ca.1900.

the National Park Act of 1930 excluded all such activity from the national parks. The cost to Rocky Mountains Park was the loss of lands at Canmore and Exshaw, and the Upper Spray Lakes. Alberta demanded these concessions as being vital to her industrial development.

The spirit of the Act is contained in its much quoted enabling clause: "The parks are hereby dedicated to the people of Canada for their benefit, education and enjoyment . . . and such parks shall be maintained and made use of so as to leave them unimpaired for the enjoyment of future generations."

Under the Act of 1930, the Dominion Parks were renamed "Canadian National Parks," and in accord with popular usage, the name Rocky Mountains Park was changed to Banff National Park. Its area was set at 7,000 square kilometres.

Harkin used his journalistic skills to publicize the parks: he wrote illustrated pamphlets to explain the purposes of the national parks, and created a Publicity and Information Division to bring the parks before the public eye in Canada and the United States.

Under Harkin's leadership, the number of parks was trebled until, by 1932, a total of eighteen parks (over 31,000 square kilometres in all) had been established across the land.

J. B. Harkin retired in 1936 after twenty-five years of uphill slogging and inspired commitment to the national parks of Canada. The full story of his achievements has yet to be written. His name is commemorated in the mountains he loved by Mount Harkin, towering above the Banff-Windermere Highway he helped see to completion in 1923.

Sibbald's Law

8

Howard Sibbald, first Chief Game Warden, 1920-1934.

*H*oward Sibbald's Law was as hard to maintain as it was easy to state: "Protect the Park." Enforcement was just a man on horseback, alone in the mountains. Distance and time were against him. There were a hundred passes and valleys that led illegal hunters into the park. The threat of fire, caused by careless campers and lightning strikes, was a constant problem. The Indians drifted through the far watersheds, following a train of thought older than any map. The park was still part of the last frontier, and frontier attitudes prevailed.

In the mind of the first chief warden, a plan took shape. He put his men to work blazing trails into the far ranges, and had them build cabins at natural crossroads in the park. In the cabins, they cached grub and fire-fighting tools. Sibbald envisioned a mobile, mounted force that would respond quickly to the smell of smoke or the sound of guns.

Fire, the great destroyer, was the main enemy in the summer months. Sibbald's fear of it, deeply rooted in the history of the park since 1885, was matched only by Commissioner Harkin's. "Eight thousand square miles of the sublimest scenery in Canada had been placed under my protection," he wrote, "and I lay awake at night thinking of the damage one bad fire might do." Sibbald's plan to divide the parks into various districts and set up a forest telephone system to the main cabins met with Harkin's approval. But the Commissioner did much more. He found an engineer in Ottawa who developed a lightweight motorized water pump that park wardens could carry by boat or packhorse in to a fire. In Banff and other parks, vehicles for highway use were fitted with hoses and pumps, and velocipedes, equipped with pumps, were used to patrol the railway lines.

Harkin put his considerable imaginative powers into a publicity campaign to prevent forest fires. Various items in constant circulation, such as axe handles, match books, and ammunition boxes, would carry a message: "Be Careful of Fires." Over the years, the number of fires and the amount of acreage burned over steadily decreased. Portable pumps, although a great improvement over buckets and wet blankets, were still awkward to pack. The hundreds of metres of linen hose were a horror to lay out in the dense shintangle and rockslides where the lightning strike invariably flares up, and, wet and stiffened, the hose was a nightmare to retrieve. Drums of gas, hand tools, food, tents — everything needed for fire fighting — went in on horseback. One spill of gas, and a horse's back would blister so badly that the animal would be disabled for weeks.

After the first snow of September, as the coyotes howled under the hunter's moon, it was time to put away the fire-fighting tools and patrol the park boundaries, watching for illegal hunters. Leaving his packhorses to graze at the headquarters cabin, the warden could ride down the river valleys into the provincial lands, then try to outflank the hunters by coming in from behind them, where they would least expect to see him. One of the first to feel Sibbald's sting was the famous Brewster outfit. One of their employees admitted to illegally shooting mountain goats in 1910. In 1912 and 1915, two of their employees were arrested and convicted of poaching mountain sheep. Other outfitters were equally guilty of flouting the law, but most were lucky enough not to get caught.

Sibbald, himself a veteran hunter and tracker, decided to fight fire with fire by hiring ex-outfitters and guides to catch up with their former colleagues. Tex Vernon-Wood, who took a fall for the Brewster outfit in 1912, was reputable enough by 1919 to pin on a badge. An earlier acquisition was Bill Peyto, who started as a part-time deputy warden in 1912. Peyto loathed the government with a passion, but he had given up outfitting after the death of his first wife and was at loose ends.

Once installed in the Healy Creek district, Bill took a personal interest in that part of the park in which one of his talc mining claims was located. Bill used to interview all newcomers to his territory, a rifle in one hand, his bloodhound, Lightning, straining at the leash in the other. Public relations was not Bill's long suit. But his presence was bad news to poachers. He and Lightning would get you if they had to track you right into the King Edward beer parlour in Banff. In his district, Peyto, like God, was omniscient. The late Jim Boyce, a grand old guide himself, told me of succumbing to temptation one summer long ago, at the sight of some big trout far up Healy Creek, the day before the season opened. "I'd just tied a string on a willow pole, just about nightfall. Just set to throw it in, when Bill stuck his head out of a bush on the other side of the creek. 'Jim,' he says, 'You'd better wait 'till tomorrow.' I said, 'Alright, Bill. I'll wait 'till tomorrow.' Then he kinda faded away and disappeared."

The first wardens were hired for their ability to ride and pack horses, handle an axe, travel on snowshoes, shoot straight, and generally take care of themselves. The Chief Warden rode over the trails occasionally to see that they were clear of deadfall, that the fire-fighting tools were in good order, the forestry phone wire was clear of trees, and plenty of firewood was put up for the winter. They were an independent and self-sufficient bunch, these oldtimers, and not adverse to talking to their horses out of loneliness. After weeks away from town with no human company, an almost telepathic relationship develops between a man and his beasts.

Sibbald with a warden and his wife at Lake Minnewanka warden cabin, ca.1920.

One October day, long ago, Warden Cyril Fuller and his horses ran into grizzly trouble at Panther Falls, north of Banff. "Arriving at the cabin," he reported, "I pulled off the packs, when the saddle horse drew my attention to something coming down the trail." The something was a grizzly bear. Just what the saddle horse had to say about it is not recorded. But it was Fuller's habit to peg rocks at the King of the Mountain when he came snooping around, and thus drive him away. This time, the technique did not work and the bear charged. Fuller had his rifle close at hand: "I was obliged to shoot him. Being head on and at such close range (sixty feet), I was unable to shoot him any other place than between the eyes, which accounts for the shattered condition of the skull."

Fuller had orders to preserve as specimens the skulls of any bears destroyed, which is why he sounds apologetic. It is very hard to hit charging grizzlies between the eyes, because they tend to move incredibly fast and toss their heads from side to side as they come in. The skull is so thick and sloped that a bullet might well glance off at any other point, with fatal results to the shooter. Duels between wardens and bears were rare in those early days, but marksmanship was a necessary skill because of the departmental policy on "noxious animals." All coyotes and wolves, for example, were to be shot on sight in order to protect "beneficial"

Fire-fighting improvements: portable horse-carried water pump (above), speeders and firetrucks (opposite left).

Opposite: Howard Sibbald with RCMP fire-fighting crew, ca.1920 (top).

Left: Howard Sibbald at home in the bush, ca.1920.

Ben Woodworth Jr. on Ptarmigan Pass hunting trip, 1920.

animals: the deer, moose, and bighorn sheep.

Although wolves were very rare in the park, the war against the coyote continued unabated for many years with local hunters' clubs setting up a howl of "wolf, wolf!" whenever the little dogs came near Banff for a sing-song. Commissioner Harkin felt that coyotes constituted a real menace to the deer. His attitude was shared by many North American parksmen at the time, including Lieutenant-Colonel Brett, Acting Superintendent of Yellowstone. He wrote Harkin in 1912 to describe the use of strychnine in killing coyotes in that park: "I have the honour to say that we make an effort to kill as many coyotes as possible each winter, and even then there are always plenty of them left . . . . Dead coyotes are sometimes found several months after the poison had been used."

To his credit, Harkin hastily proscribed any use of poison in the Canadian parks. The wardens were to continue to shoot coyotes, however, and each man would have a quota established. Unfortunately for the wardens, coyotes tend to hunt at night.

Harkin, who was the kind of administrator that had his finger on everything, from the building of a new highway to the purchase of laundry soap, had the solution for his coyote hunters. He sent them a recipe for coyote lure: "Put into a bottle the urine from a coyote, the gall and anal glands . . . . For four ounces of mixture, use one-quarter the amount of glycerine to give it body." He suggested the men should conceal themselves under an elk hide rubbed with the above fetor, until the coyotes, feeling either truculent or romantic, should venture near. Wardens W. Neish and R. D. Barnetson, two oldtime "bush apes," as the wardens sometimes called themselves, drily reported that "the scent from a hidden warden would dominate over that of the bait offered."

The wardens killed thirty to fifty coyotes every year without making serious inroads on their numbers until, in 1937, dead coyotes started cropping up all over

Bill Peyto by his cabin at Simpson Summit, 1913. "In his district, Peyto was omniscient."

the park. According to the park superintendent, "Innoculation of coyotes with mange germs, and then turning them loose to infect others, practised by the U.S. parks in late years, was affecting the animals across the border." Sometimes I think that the coyote, rather than the beaver, should be the symbol on the modern warden's hat badge, as a reminder of this absurd and barbaric campaign against old *coyotle*, the trickster god of Amerindian mythologies.

The coyote war was part of a long campaign against all predators in the national parks, which can be traced back to W. F. Whitcher's advice to destroy all "lupine, vulpine, and feline vermin," back in 1886. Whitcher's misguided kernel of "wisdom" bore bitter fruit in the thirties. The fecundity of the park elk herd (reintroduced into the park in 1917-1920) and the lack of natural predators (wolves) combined to display man's ignorance of predator-prey relationships.

The elk is a formidable competitor for grazing rights among the ungulates. By 1933, the park deer herds were beginning to show the effects of the slim pickings left by the elk, and Commissioner Harkin was having second thoughts about killing predators. "Large parks," he told his superintendents, "are sufficiently large to permit nature to control the numbers of animals within their boundaries." But wardens were still to shoot "wolves, wolverines, coyotes, and cougars" seen chasing big game. "It is not the policy, however, to organize any special onslaught upon any of the predatory animals."

But his enlightenment came too late. By 1937, the elk herd was so large that the native deer and bighorn sheep were literally starving to death. The wardens were then ordered to reduce the herd by shooting, a practice that continued for several decades. Imbalances between prey and predators in Yellowstone Park created the same situation there.

After 1933, the campaign against predators was slowly wound down. The coyotes, prolific breeders, returned to serenade the burghers of Banff and raid the garbage cans late at night. Eventually, a small pack of wolves, the real article, returned to the park, wisely confining their hunting to the remote north boundary. They brought an aura of romantic savagery back to the wilderness.

Howard Sibbald moved up to a park superintendency in Kootenay National Park, but Sibbald's Law, "Protect the Park," remains one of the first duties of the Warden Service.

As the world outside grew more and more into a concrete maze, as the numbers of visitors swelled year by year, the third generation of wardens would learn their next great task. It was to protect the people, who, out of inexperience, confusion, or recklessness, made the mistake of underestimating the cruel indifference the mountains have always shown to human frailties.

Between the Wars

9

*I*n 1915, the reality of the Great War, which had sent visitation into a nose dive, intruded to the very heart of the national park. Armed guards paced the roadway near Painter's stone-faced belvederes. High fences topped with barbed wire shone wickedly in the winter light, cheapening and degrading the peaceful grandeur of the new building.

The barbed wire ringed a temporary barracks that housed "enemy aliens." These enemies were in fact a group of immigrants, mainly of Austro-Hungarian origin, who had been rounded up from across the country and interned as possible "saboteurs." Most of them were innocent of any hostile intention towards their adopted land. They spent the winter clearing land for the subdivision that now makes up the exclusive St. Julien Road. During the summer, they camped at Castle Mountain and worked on building the highway to Lake Louise, now known as the Bow Valley Parkway.

Overleaf: Swiss guides, ca.1915.

World War I alien internment camp near Cave and Basin, ca.1918.

The Beehive and Bridal Falls, Canadian Rockies

BEEHIVE
Tea Room

Highest situated
Tea Room in
Canada

MENU

Luncheon $1.25

Roast Sirloin of Beef,
Corn Pudding.
Mashed Potatoes.

Cold Roast Beef & Salad.

Hot Biscuit & Honey

Lemon Snow Pudding

Tea or Coffee.

Commissioner Harkin was glad to have their help, involuntary or not, and arranged for more camps to keep park development moving. The nation's energy was focused on winning the war, and there was little money or manpower left for "frills" like national parks.

Bill Peyto was among the Banffites who went to war. He returned from Europe in 1918 with a chunk of flesh missing from his thigh, and memories of friends who had died beside him. The nation, bitterly wounded, lost over 60,000 of its finest young men in the stinking trenches of the Old World.

As if anxious to enjoy what had been denied to so many, North Americans turned to the parks in record numbers in the twenties. In 1923 the Banff-Windermere Highway, following in the steps of Dr. Hector's route of 1858, was officially opened. It gave motor access to the West Coast, and to the national parks in the U.S. But the highways of the twenties were narrow, and poorly gravelled. Washouts and mudholes turned them into obstacle courses that only the most innovative motorists could transcend. Most tourists were funnelled into Banff through the Canadian Pacific Railway's rail and steamship system, "the world's greatest," the company proudly claimed. The railroad continued its policy of hiring talented photographers and artists, bringing them west to capture the scenery. Their work was used in brochures and posters advertising the mountains.

The CPR's infallible crystal ball had already foreseen the ultimate winner of the contest between trains and automobiles. In 1922-24, they built bungalow camps at Storm Mountain and Moraine Lake, aimed specifically at the new class of traveller. These "motels" collected motorists' dollars. The loose change of those venturesome souls who dared to walk a few kilometres was deftly snared by the corporation in several charming tea houses, one of which still survives above Lake Louise. These were in accord with the railroad's portrayal of the Rockies as "the Canadian Switzerland."

This Swiss theme was exemplified in the flesh by the railroad's colourful Swiss mountain guides, who had been brought to the Rockies to guide the tourist mountaineers, after the death of mountaineer Philip Stanley Abbot, in 1896. It would take another book to record the exploits of these men. For many years, their headquarters during the summer was the guides' chalet beside Chateau Lake Louise. Their monument is Abbot's Hut, a refuge for climbers perched on a desolate col on the Great Divide above Lake Louise. It is built after the Swiss style, of native limestone quarried on the site. The guides themselves hauled water from a glacial stream nearby to make the mortar.

If the CPR welcomed the motorists who frequented their new bungalow camps, they were less thrilled at the car campers who thronged the first campground next

Above: Abbot's Hut, a longtime refuge for climbers on the Great Divide.

Upper left: Summit of Pinnacle Peak, near Moraine Lake, 1919.

Lower left: Packtrain near Abbot Pass toting supplies for construction of Abbot's Hut, 1922.

to the Banff Springs golf course. There were complaints about snotty urchins scampering across the fairways, spoiling one's game. Towels and underwear, hung out to dry, flapped vulgarly at distinguished duffers from far distant lands. After bargaining with Harkin, the problem was finally solved. The government built a new campground at Tunnel Mountain, which would become the main campsite in the park.

The mud and horsedung that had afflicted the first tourists gave way to the more modern stink of car exhaust. Jim Brewster, one of the farsighted businessmen of Banff, had the first touring cars in the park, and took the visitors on cacophonous jaunts over rocky Tunnel Mountain Drive and up to Lake Minnewanka. Steam launches plied "the Lake-Where-Some-Spirit-Being-Dwells."

There was a fish hatchery on the Spray River, supplying fry to be released in the park streams for the benefit of the angler; there was a zoo and aviary with its exotic wildlife; there was the fanciful Banff Springs Hotel. If you couldn't afford to stay in it, you could at least go and gawk at it. In the Hotel, the blur of crochet hooks had given way to flying champagne corks, as the dowagers of the great pre-war imperialists gave way to the flappers of the twenties and the fashion plates of the thirties. "The men played golf," as one writer put it, "while the women changed their clothes." The grand hotel had entered what its chronicler, Bart Robinson, has called its "brief, but golden moment." Its ballrooms were thronged with princes, movie stars, and maharajahs. The hotel and the town were world famous.

To titillate these potentates, the original owners of the mountains came back each year to their ancient campground near the foot of Cascade Mountain. During Banff Indian Days, they paraded through the town with painted faces on painted horses to the grand hotel. There they sang the old mountain songs, and danced the old stories, thrilling the uncomprehending hearts of the white usurpers.

The central attraction, for the less wealthy tourists, was still the hot springs. Banff had 79,000 visitors in 1922, and 49,000 of them visited the Cave and Basin. A pleasant pine-scented walk up Cave Avenue, rather than a noisy auto ride to the pool, became a local tradition of the Banff residents and was soon preferred by many returning tourists.

Banff, in short, had everything needed to divert the tourists and to attract as many people as possible. The policy of the parks branch and of the businessmen seemed one and the same.

But as the motorists increased, there was trouble with fires along the roads, with panhandling black and grizzly bears, and with the occasional sodbuster shooting a deer to take home in his rumble seat. On weekends, the town warden, responsible for impounding dogs and dusting truculent black bears with a load of number six shotgun pellets, would have to call in a few bush-apes to lend him a hand with fires or bear trouble. It soon became necessary to train this backcountry cavalry in the driving of the automobile. The technique was simple: the bowlegged novice was installed in a battered Ford at the warden horse corral. He then drove around with much grinding of gears and caroming off corral posts until the other wardens, perched on the rails to watch the contest, stopped cheering. At that point, the gate was opened and the triumphant tyro was turned loose on an unsuspecting public.

Banff and the Bow Valley now belonged to the masses, but many of the ''mink and manure set'' had outgrown their fling with the automobile and returned to the saddle. In 1925 the Banff Advisory Council (the town has never had a mayor or alderman) petitioned the superintendent for more bridle paths. These were for the use of the ''wealthy classes'' which ''form so great a portion of our summer visitors.'' They wanted trails to points that were ''inaccessible by motor.''

Up until the twenties, the wardens met few people, other than passing hunting parties, while on their solitary patrols. One group that did penetrate the wilderness every summer was the Alpine Club of Canada, founded in 1906, and aided, of course, by the CPR.

The CPR

Was everywhar.

Not surprisingly, it was a CPR man, John Murray Gibbon, who helped to get the public exploring the hundreds of hectares of park wilderness. Gibbon, who was a CPR publicity agent, took a liking to trail riding after a trip with Tom Wilson in 1909. Gibbon and some friends on that trip were instrumental in founding the Trail Riders of the Canadian Rockies in 1924. The idea was to encourage Canadians to explore their own wilderness, support the conservation of animal life, and improve the trail system in the parks. The success of the Trail Riders led to the formation of a pedestrian contingent, the Skyline Hikers, in 1933.

With the coming of Gibbon, whose activities were favoured by Commissioner Harkin and the CPR, the warden service was put to work improving trails along the proposed route of the riders and hikers. The clubs were self-contained groups of people, with experienced guides. But quaint hand-hewn bridges and stretches of corduroy looked safer to green riders than swollen rivers and bottomless muskeg. The wardens kept in the background and kept an eye peeled. Large parties of people too often meant large piles of garbage, causing nocturnal visits from black and grizzly bears. The park superintendent didn't want any nasty encounters with the park fauna spoiling the press releases which followed the rides and hikes; neither did Commissioner Harkin.

Clearing of Banff-Windermere Hwy., ca. 1923.

Above: At the Cave and Basin, 1922.

Upper left: Banff Winter Carnival, 1925.

Lower left: In 1928, feeding the bears was still a novelty, but the bears soon became a grave problem.

Opposite: Wilf Carter serenades the ladies on a Trail Riders of the Canadian Rockies trip, 1935 (left).
Chateau Lake Louise pool, ca.1930 (right).

Erling Strom, ca.1932.

The man who gave his blessing to the first Trail Rider camp was Tom Wilson, the old trailblazer. He was a bit overwhelmed to see 207 dudes on horseback all at once. Speeches of welcome were made, but according to Ted Hart's account in *The Selling of Canada,* Wilson's reply was brief: "I am not accustomed to extemporaneous speaking," he allowed, "unless a cayuse has stepped upon my foot." Wilson was more voluble, however, when he met one of Banff's first ski entrepreneurs a few years later. Walking down Banff Avenue, Wilson encountered Erling Strom, a young Norwegian ski instructor. Strom had come to Banff with an Italian nobleman-cum-mountain-guide, the Marquis degli Albizzi, and four clients, to make the first winter journey to Mount Assiniboine. Strom would later establish a ski lodge there, in cooperation with the CPR.

Wilson looked the young skier over and declared, "There ought to be 'open season' on people like you." Wilson believed Strom would lose his dudes in an avalanche or get them frozen to death.

Strom was no shrinking violet, however. He proudly told the old horseman, "We are winter people . . . we think that snow opens the country." His reply proved prophetic for the thousands of cross-country skiers who now visit the national parks every winter.

The beginnings of Banff's multi-million dollar ski industry can be traced back beyond Strom's first trip, to some local boys with home-made skis and leather bindings, who built a jump for the first Banff Winter Carnival in 1917. By 1937 the sport was so popular that the CPR began running special "Snow Trains" to bring the skiers and spectators to the mountains.

One group that was slow to take to the heavy hickories was the warden service. Since the wardens usually travelled alone, they preferred to lumber along their solitary paths on snowshoes, which they regarded as safer and more efficient than skis. One notable exception in Banff Park was Jack Romansen, who patrolled the Bryant Creek district near Mount Assiniboine on skis. Romansen was an innovator who scorned the use of ski wax or climbing skins for uphill plodding. He had some kind of hinge mechanism bolted to the tail of his skis to keep him from slipping backwards. Romansen used the high winds on Spray Lake to his advantage when travelling eastward. He had a parachute, which he used to unfurl on arrival at the lake, which moved him forward at breakneck speed when a chinook wind was blowing. According to legend a workman from Calgary Power drove his truck into the ditch one day when, upon looking out the window, he saw Romansen sailing past him suspended from a parachute some fifteen metres above the ice, headed east.

Skiing, without benefit of ski lifts, continued to grow in popularity among the locals during the Great Depression of the thirties. Dollars were in short supply, but snow was plentiful and free. The main centres were Mount Norquay and Sunshine near Banff, and Skoki Lodge, near Lake Louise.

As the Depression continued, the summer mountains once again became the preserve of the rich. To many Westerners, like the parched Alberta farmers, the shining mountains were only mirages on the horizon, memories of green forests and blue running water. They waited for the dark clouds to form over them, and bring the rain they desperately needed for their drought-stricken crops. In the park of 1935, businessmen built new bungalow camps; in Saskatchewan, the police broke young workers' heads in the Regina Riot. The CPR planted special grass for their golf course and fenced it away from the insatiable elk; the sprinklers whirred in the sunlight.

Speeding west on a crack passenger train, the wealthy tourists were occasionally alarmed to be slowed by a horde of grasshoppers so thick that the driving wheels slipped and lost traction on the greasy rails. But the freight trains carried another class of tourists; an entire generation of young, unemployed working men roamed restlessly across the country, riding the rods. In Banff they found jobs of sorts on relief projects. The Upper Hot Springs bathhouse was built in 1932 by local unemployed workers, as was the handbuilt Norquay Road, and part of the Banff-Jasper Highway. And when Benny Goodman requested an airport be built at Banff, so he could fly in in his private plane in 1934, the CPR had a word with the government and the young men went to work at the foot of Cascade Mountain with axe and shovel.

Then Hitler marched into Poland and before long everybody had a job, either making guns or carrying them into battle. The great hotel closed in 1942 for the duration of the war. Gas was rationed, and tourism shot. But on weekends, winter and summer, the trains brought uniformed men and women on leave, determined to enjoy themselves while they still had a chance.

The highminded clause of the 1930 National Parks Act, that the parks would remain "unimpaired for future generations" was about to be tested to the limit. With the end of World War II, the parks entered a period of popularity beyond the wildest dreams of their great architect, J. B. Harkin. "The parks belong to the people," he once said. Now, the people, in unprecedented numbers, were about to come and see what the parks had to offer, each with a different expectation. The fight to make the first "nation's park" a success was won before the Commissioner retired; the struggle to save the park from its own success was about to begin.

Skiing at Sunshine, ca.1937.

*T*he bighorn ram was heavy, like any dead animal, and the sun had been working on it. Whoever had run it down was travelling many kilometres over the speed limit; every bone in its body was broken.

I took a deep breath, grabbed one horn, and skidded the bloody mess up the plank into the back of the patrol truck. It was my first summer as a warden in Banff National Park. I'd spent the winter on the west boundary of Prince Albert National Park in Saskatchewan, listening to the wolves howling and hadn't seen a tourist for six months.

"Welcome to Banff," they'd said when I reported to my new assignment early that spring. "You finally made the Big Time." The radio crackled and chattered over the noise of passing cars, as I slid in behind the wheel. The Big Time was very busy, and the Big Time had problems. It was chock-a-block on that sunny day with people and with stopped-up toilets, traffic jams, lost hikers, and hungry black bears. Most of my own mob were busy with a helicopter sling rescue on the cliffs of Mt. Rundle. One climber was dead and one was hanging on with trembling fingers.

As I pulled out into the traffic I heard the attendant at the overflow campground calling my dispatcher. She sounded worried. "Where's that squad car? Over."

"RCMP are tied up with a motor vehicle accident. Over."

"Well, send us some help please, before they lynch this guy!"

"Stand by, thirty-five. Fifty-nine, Warden Office."

I picked up the microphone. "Fifty-nine. I copied. I'm on the way." The overflow campground was in fact an abandoned gravel pit, lined cheek to jowl with behemoth motorhomes and trailers. I pulled up beside the attendant's truck. There was a small knot of angry middle-aged fathers of young children talking to the attendant. The focus of their attention was a male caucasian of tender years. He was obviously very drunk and at that moment was draped around a pine tree, publicly urinating, and yelling, *"Harvey, Harvey, where the hell are ya Harvey?"*

Harvey had been run out of the campground earlier that morning after a noisy party was broken up by the police. But this kid had passed out in the bushes, and was left behind. The harried attendant came over. "Will you puh-lease get this guy outta here," she said. "He's really grossing everybody out."

I led the boy to the truck. He smelled worse than the dead sheep. Dazedly, he climbed in.

126

"Do up your seatbelt, please."

"Where the hell am I?"

"Welcome to Banff National Park," I told him. "You're under arrest."

"I feel SICK!"

"Well, roll down the window!"

Dead animals, traffic jams, gravel pits, and drunks — what's all this about, anyway? The short-term answer is "popularity."

Post-war prosperity and the post-war baby boom had caught up with the national parks. The crowds rolled in on rubber wheels, and the railroad gave way to the automobile as the most popular form of travel to the parks. By 1960, there was a passenger car for every 4.5 Canadians. Mom, Dad, Dick and Jane, and the half-sized Canadian chewing on a pacifier, were part of the one million visitors to Banff National Park that year. By 1966, the numbers reached two million and park facilities were strained to overflowing.

During the sixties and seventies the Trans-Canada Highway became a killing ground for park wildlife, and the mix of high-speed transport trucks and slow-moving tourist vehicles led to an increasing number of human tragedies. As this book goes to press, the Trans-Canada Highway is being twinned. For the first time, fences and underpasses are in use to protect the wildlife from the automobile. These are bitter but necessary compromises between safety and national park ideals. We have learned much from them: we have learned that highways, like railroads, have no place in the national parks of the future.

Let me hasten to add that all these regrettable things are happening in a very narrow strip of land, the Bow Corridor of the park. There are some 6,000 square kilometres of relatively unspoiled back country that lie on either side of the railroad and highway. Unfortunately, it is this corridor that serves as the introduction to the park for all its visitors, and it is here that many of them choose to stay.

So there is still wilderness, thanks be to Howard Douglas, et al. But there will always be the highway, the railroad, the ski lifts, and above all, beautiful metro Banff, set like a neon spider in this web of steel and asphalt. In what other town in Canada can you ride a gondola lift, go downhill or cross-country skiing, thrill to the roar of transport trucks, photograph a moose, eat a gourmet meal, soak in nature's own hot tub, see the Royal Winnipeg Ballet perform live, get drunk, boogie till you drop, and collect a parking ticket, all in one fun-filled day?

Nowhere. That's the trouble. But you can do some of these things quite happily in any city, minus only the scenic backdrop of high mountains. National parks, however, are supposed to offer us a quieter, more contemplative experience, one that can be had nowhere else except within their sacred precincts. Yes, everybody

Main Street, Banff, 1913 and today.

Aileen Harmon near Mt. Assiniboine, 1934.

has heard of Banff. But it's surprising how many Canadians (about 65%, according to one poll) are not aware that the town is located in a national park. I wonder why that is?

For too many years, the first national park tried to be all things to all people, as the willing bride of free enterprise. Everybody tipped their hats to the noble sentiment of "preserving the national parks unimpaired for future generations." Just how this was to be done was not effectively answered. And what one person sees as impairment, looks like wondrous improvement to another. Some were horrified to see a single wildflower picked. To others, man-made structures, like ski-lift towers and "attractions" such as Banff's famous wax museum, offered spectacles unparalleled in nature. The house of wax is no longer with us. But there are now three major ski hills in our first national park. Some Banff boosters see the park as the "jet-set playground of the future," if only Parks Canada would allow more expansion.

Decades ago, Commissioner Harkin warned us that "the parks may lose the very thing that distinguished them from the outside world," unless development was strictly controlled. That has come true in spades. As a member of the International Union for the Conservation of Nature (IUCN), Canada, with the largest park system in the world, helped to set international standards for reserving new parks. These guidelines excluded "inhabited and exploited areas" from being designated as national parks. Sadly, and ironically for Canada, our first national park has been cited as one which no longer measures up to those very requirements.

Obviously, our first national park has been the victim of history, and the tremendous pressures put on it over the years by the visiting public and by businessmen pressing for expanded facilities. Within the parks service, anonymous public servants fought to preserve national and historic parks in the face of public apathy. The parks were popular, but taken for granted by those who used them. At the same time, park policy evolved in a piecemeal fashion, and without the benefit of sound ecological consideration for managing landscape and wildlife.

In 1960, the Honourable Alvin Hamilton, then Minister in charge of the Parks Branch, made a desperate appeal in Parliament. He asked for people who loved the parks to "band together," and support the Minister to help save the parks from those who wished to exploit them with "every honky-tonk recreational device known to man." The Parks Branch was by then undergoing an internal revolution to create, for the first time, a comprehensive management policy that would undo some of the mistakes of the past, and safeguard the new parks of the future. Concerned citizens and conservation groups, like the National and Provincial Parks Association, rallied to the cause. They helped to publicize the need for more parks, and the need to control urban-type recreational facilities in the parks.

The Parks Branch entered the Age of Aquarius with an ambitious goal that reflected the public's desire for more national parks, parks that would represent each of the country's forty-eight natural life zones. Parks were proposed for the Arctic, for the Atlantic and Pacific coastlines, and for the Prairie grasslands. The goal expressed in 1964 is a big one: "to identify a new system of parks which is representative of Canada's natural and human heritage, to preserve the parks for all time . . . ." It has been given concrete form in the ten national parks established since 1964, parks like Kejimkujik in Nova Scotia, Pacific Rim on Vancouver Island, and three northern parks, Nahanni, Kluane, and Auyuittuq. Others are on the drawing board. But making national parks is a long and difficult process, unlike the days when the Minister of the Interior had the power to unilaterally set land aside as park reserves. It may take eight years to complete the research and negotiations with provincial governments and citizens, before landscapes (or historic sites) of national interest can be acquired by the federal government.

In all national parks, inventories of the life forms, landscapes, historic features, and ecologically sensitive habitat were to be made by scientists. A land use system would then be set up to zone the park lands into, for example, "outdoor recreation areas," "special areas" (sensitive habitat), and "intensive use areas" (townsite and service areas). On the basis of factual knowledge and appropriate zoning, type of visitor activities and the intensity of those activities could then be controlled. The idea was to keep man's use of the parks in harmonious balance with the other life forms the parks were set up to protect.

By means of the public hearing process, the people were invited to play their part in planning the future of their parks. The key to setting parks aside, and protecting them afterwards, is an enlightened populace. Education of the public has long been a central purpose of the national parks but, until 1959, Canada lagged well behind the United States in the area of park interpretation.

That year marked the founding of the National Parks Interpretive Service. The first park naturalists (or park interpreters, as they are often known) seemed an ethereal crew to the blood-and-guts veterans of the park warden service. My first important encounter with a naturalist in action happened near Parker Ridge, on the Banff-Jasper Highway. My attention was caught by a group of people huddled around a gesticulating figure dressed in an orange anorak. It was a blustery day with the feel of sleet in it: the summer was nearly over.

Curious, I walked over and was greeted by a group of smiling tourists evidently enjoying themselves. The man in the anorak was seasonal naturalist, Bob Sandford. In lieu of a uniform hat, he was wearing a white chef's cap.

"You're just in time," he cried jovially. "We're creating the earth." Mystified,

Skiing at Skoki.

Overleaf: Lower Pika Peak, Skoki Valley region.

I stared at the paraphernalia he had set on a folding camp table: two large baking pans, buckets of sand, a spray bottle full of water, a can of flour, a jar of parsley flakes, and a can of lemon-scented shaving cream.

He began by pouring a little wood alcohol into one his baking pans. "In the beginning there was nothing," he intoned sepulchrally. A hush fell over the group; they were mesmerized by the inspired glint in his eyes. "Only a void of blackness in which I beheld infinity. I stirred it with fire to amuse myself!" he cried, and ignited the alcohol with a flick of his Bic. "I created flaming matter!" he crowed, stirring in some sand with a large wooden spoon. The tray was transformed into a burning Christmas pudding, to the delight of the youngsters.

The cosmic cook picked up a wooden spoon and ladled some steaming sand into the other pan. "I made the earth," he told us. "On the seventh day I rested, and let 'er cool off."

As we watched, enthralled, he shaped the sand into a dome to create the globe's hot surface. With a few airy gestures he sketched in some clouds. With the spray bottle he made some river beds, managing to wet some of the spectators in the process. A bucket of water produced the ocean: a can of sardines became the first marine life. The ocean, filled with the sediment of teeming marine life, dried up. The layers of sediment, uplifted by spatula, faulted and buckled into mountains under the sculptor's hand. Some of the children looked up at the mountains around them and seemed to see them for the first time.

Then it snowed flour, and the flour compressed to form creamy, lemon-scented glaciers. The glaciers oozed down the mountainsides, carving out hanging valleys and levelling the land into prairies. Bob gave the Ice Age a sunny smile and the ice retreated into the high peaks. Parsley flakes grew into grass and trees, and the mountain earth was complete.

"But how does anything really grow in all this rock and ice?" asked one lady as she turned from the scale model to the high, glaciated peaks of the Great Divide towering around them.

"Let me show you something," said Bob, putting on his Stetson again. He led us to a lichen-covered boulder, set around with white heather bells. "Here is one of the places where life begins. This red scaly growth is a living plant, a lichen. It's the product of a union between a fungus and an algae. The fungus retains water that the algae needs to grow. The algae produces a carbohydrate because it has the chlorophyll the fungus lacks, which makes photosynthesis possible.

"Science calls this union of plants a symbiotic relationship. I call it the green kiss of life. This lichen is one of the first building blocks of life. Eventually, thousands of years from now, it will have dissolved this boulder; it will have created the soil in which this small white-flowered heather can grow, in which those stunted alpine firs over there can be nurtured.''

''It's a slow process,'' observed one of the listeners.

''Yes indeed,'' said the naturalist. ''It takes thousands of years to make soil on these slopes that is only a few inches thick. The whole life of the mountains depends on those few inches of soil. That's why we have to be so careful with how we treat the mountain earth — where we put roads, campgrounds, ski lifts, even hiking trails.''

I was impressed with the way this crafty flower sniffer had entertained the park visitors. It became clear that it was only a means of conveying, in a large spirited way, a very important message.

Bob Sandford took his job very seriously indeed. He once described the park naturalist as ''the human link between the cultural and historical elements in the landscape, and the park visitor.'' The park naturalists supplement their guided hikes with programmes designed to explain the park features. Sandford used banks of slide projectors, poems, original songs, and taped interviews with oldtimers to make the park come alive in the visitors' imaginations.

The naturalists arrived on the scene not a moment too soon. Much depends on their ability to change the Disneyland attitude toward landscape and wildlife that afflicts many urbanized park visitors. In the national parks, this attitude is most manifest in the public's predilection for hand-feeding wild animals, a dangerous and illegal practice. More and more wild animals, especially black bears, turned into snack-food junkies over the years. The handouts, and the presence of large quantities of garbage in the townsite and campgrounds, conditioned black and grizzly bears to the presence of man. Such conditioned animals are twice as dangerous to humans because we tend to see them as ''tame'' bears and treat them accordingly — without respect.

The warden service spent more and more time, over the years, setting ''culvert'' traps for garbage bears, or tranquilizing and relocating them by truck or helicopter into the back country. Repeat offenders were destroyed as a last resort, which makes inroads into the bear population. Autopsies sometimes showed their stomachs to be diseased, clogged with wads of plastic bags.

In 1980, when several people were mauled (one fatally) by a grizzly bear a few hundred metres from the town limits, grim reality caught up with past errors. Garbage handling policy in the park is now drastically changed and garbage is now trucked to Calgary for disposal. Despite an information campaign in the park and in the media, some people persist in feeding wildlife.

Although Parks Canada counts heavily on its interpreters to explain park values,

Swiss guides, ca.1904.

it is still up to the warden service to enforce regulations; to save the parks from abuse, and protect the people from hazards in the parks. Today's warden, usually a technical school graduate in Resource Conservation (many are university graduates), is a product of past traditions and present-day realities. The Stetson that he or she wears recalls the small band of cowboys Howard Sibbald hired in 1909. Though wardens in the western parks still patrol with saddle and pack horses, their counterparts in the coastal parks have had to learn how to plot a ship's course and dive with scuba gear, in order to protect a much different environment.

The mountain wardens have had to keep pace with the outdoor recreation boom after World War II. About 1950, the warden service was forced to admit that the ski and the ski lift were the wave of the future. They learned how to ski just in time to run the first ski patrols, and they learned how to forecast avalanches, lead avalanche rescue teams, and stabilize ski slopes with high explosives.

The need to turn the cowboy skiers into all-round mountaineers was underlined by a terrible climbing accident on Mount Victoria, near Lake Louise, in July of 1954. Four Mexican women climbers and their male guide fell six hundred metres to their deaths in Abbot Pass. Three terrified women, climbing on a separate rope, were stranded on the mountain. Swiss guide Ernest Feuz, then sixty-five years old, led the rescue party of Canadian Pacific Railway staff. He made the ascent in half the normal time required.

Climbing and skiing accidents had been a rarity before World War II. Although the Parks Branch always had the responsibility for rescue work, most rescues above the treeline had been carried out by the Swiss guides or members of the Alpine Club. The wardens had assisted by packing out the few casualties on tobbogans in winter, and by horse-slung stretchers in the summer. But by 1955 Ernest Feuz was due to retire, and the CPR had decided to dispense with their guide service.

National Parks Director James A. Hutchinson viewed the loss of the Swiss guides with alarm, and determined that training must begin at once to turn the warden service of the various mountain parks into a competent mountain rescue group. Walter Perren, a thirty-seven-year-old Swiss guide, was hired to undertake the task and was made Chief Warden in charge of mountain rescue training, based in Banff. He faced a cavalry outfit. The attitude towards mountain climbers held by some grizzled veterans of the service was one of frank hostility.

"I can get any dumb s.o.b. down off any mountain around here — with a .270," was how one oldtimer expressed it.

Nevertheless, the patient, smiling Swiss powerhouse, Perren, won the confidence of the oldtimers without exception. At the first climbing school, held at "Cuthead College," a tent camp north of Banff, he amazed his charges by scampering up

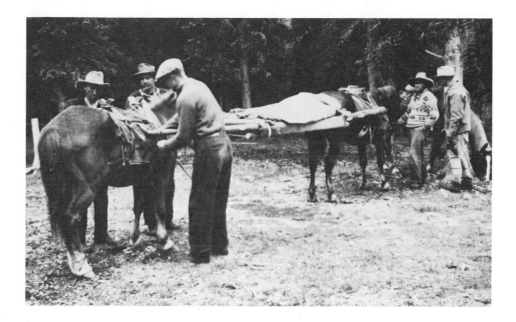

Rescue on horse-slung stretcher.

rly years at the Cave and Basin.

I passed the tobacco pouch to Jim, feeling like a leper in my park uniform, as he filled his pipe in morose silence. Every time I walked down Banff Avenue, little kids would come up and ask me, "How come you closed down the swimming pool?" as if it were my personal decision. Just about everybody in Banff had learned to swim at the old pool.

There had been a lot of good reasons for the decision, of course. Ever since 1916, subsidence, due to the unstable rock, had caused cracks in the pool and part of the structure. Health regulations required chlorination of the water in 1960: pink-eye had become a problem in the warm pool. But chlorination made for an unsightly and unsafe white sediment in the water which resulted in the closing of the warm pools, and the use of non-mineral water in the big pool.

Visitation declined steadily over the years. The climate in the mountains works against cold-water swimming except on the very hottest days. Without the warm pools, there was no more "shoulder season" to keep the revenue up on pool use. It became clear that nothing short of major renovations could stop the rain of ceiling plaster and the cracks in the structure. The place was a public hazard, and renovation would be very costly. Painter's old masterpiece had done well by the national park. Now she was out to pasture behind her plywood blinkers until the powers that be decided just what to do with her.

and down the cliffs like a mountain goat as they clung and clawed at the crumbling holds, learning the ropes.

In those days, nine out of ten wardens were devoted to nicotine. "Walter," some poor smoker would wheeze, with a butt dangling from his lower lip, "how much further is it?" Then high above, where the nylon rope led to some tiny belay stance, the guide's head would poke out into space, smiling down at them.

"It's chust a liddle bit up," he would call encouragingly.

"Chust a liddle bit up," they would mutter angrily; the answer was always the same, whether it was a 200-metre practice cliff, or an "11,000-footer," studded with ice. "Chust a liddle bit up" became their humorous and painful rallying cry.

One of Walter's favourite finishing schools for climbers was Mount Victoria. There is a famous sickle of snow on the south ridge with nothing above it but clouds, and nothing below it but British Columbia on the one hand, and Alberta on the other. Walter used to stroll across this spidery catwalk with the rope playing out behind him, find a good belay spot, and cry out, "Ho-kay, boys." The novice climbers would often take to straddling the nasty thing, inching across on their frozen buns.

"Stand up, boys," said Walter cheerfully. "You won't bump your heads." And the cowboy climbers suddenly realized they had just climbed their first high mountain. It made them smile, despite themselves; some of them actually enjoyed it but they managed to keep that to themselves.

To keep pace with developments in mountaineering, the wardens began to train for longer periods of time, using more sophisticated equipment. They practised with the first cable rescue gear developed in Switzerland and, in 1966, used it to lift two stranded climbers from a ledge eighty metres below the summit of Mount Babel (3,101 m.).

Walter Perren succeeded in transforming the park wardens into a capable band of mountaineers. His untimely death in 1967 from leukemia robbed the warden service of their greatest guide, and robbed the mountaineering public of a truly benevolent spirit who was happiest with lots of altitude under his feet. By 1975, when the Banff warden service carried out a record 134 rescues in one year, mountaineering was all in a day's work.

In the last decade, proficiency in mountain rescue has led to Parks Canada's inclusion as the only North American member of ICAR, the International Commission of Alpine Rescue. Much of the credit must go to Walter Perren's successors, Peter Fuhrmann of Banff Park, and Willi Pfisterer of Jasper, regional alpine specialists.

Fuhrmann and Pfisterer have worked aggressively over the years to maintain and improve on international standards for rescue introduced by Perren. Fuhrmann introduced the helicopter sling rescue technique to the parks. This involves slinging one or two wardens in a special harness beneath a helicopter to reach accident sites where the machine cannot land due to the steep terrain.

With the recruiting of wardens from younger generations, the attitude of the service to mountaineering has changed dramatically. A number of wardens have qualified for membership in the Association of Canadian Mountain Guides. Climbing, like skiing, whether downhill, cross-country, or with alpine touring skis, is an established part of the job, all part of life in the Big Time.

O ne summer day in 1978, I left the warden office and drove up towards Sundance Canyon on patrol. At the Cave and Basin, an oldtimer I knew (I'll call him Jim) flagged me down, and I pulled over to shoot the breeze with him.

Time had not been kind to Painter's masterpiece. The Cave was no longer the main park attraction to the more sophisticated visitors of our era. The pool was closed, its glass windshields covered with plywood. Those who wished to soak in sulphur water would now have to go to the Upper Hot Springs. It was eerily silent, except for a couple of ravens yacking away. Their voices echoed from the bottom of the empty swimming pool. Vandals had been at work, and bits of broken glass crunched underfoot as I walked over to where the old man sat on the steps of the belvederes.

"Jim, how you been keepin'?"

"Pretty good 'till I come up and seen this mess. What the hell's goin' on? See you got the sun on your face," he added before I could answer. "Ain't been a half-ton jockey all summer, maybe?"

I sat down beside him and began to fill my pipe. "Just came out of the Dormer River," I told him. "Ten-day patrol. Wish I was still there."

His face lit up. He was probably remembering a few bighorns he had poached out there before I was born. "That big shale slope at the summit . . . . ''

"Yes?"

"Any goat there?"

"Ten or twelve, every time I ride through there."

"That's something, ain't it?" he said with a smile. "Like you could reach across from the saddle and pull an old billy's beard as you go by . . . . ''

"Except for the canyon right under your left foot."

"Glad to hear they're still there," he said softly.

"No thanks to you."

"Ha!" He slapped his leg and grinned. "You know I got too stove up to ride . . . know how old I am? Eighty. But I can still swim." He was silent for a few seconds.

"I come up here to swim, only pool in town you can swim in. And you shut her down."

"Jim, I didn't . . . . ''

"Shut her down," he muttered angrily.

"They give the old place a real facelift back in the late fifties," Jim allowed, "but they should have done some major rebuilding then."

I nodded. "There's just no money for that kind of reconstruction right now. You know, it's kind of questionable if a swimming pool is really appropriate in a national park," I added, lamely.

Jim snorted smoke and yanked the pipe out of his mouth. "Tell it to the ski lifts!" he said sharply.

I sucked unhappily on my own incinerator, silenced by the usual Banff conundrum: on the one hand, grizzly bears; on the other hand, disco city.

"So what are ya gonna do, just let the whole damn place sink into the muck?" demanded Jim.

"Well, it's not up to . . .," I began, and sighed. The pipe wouldn't stay lit; I put it away. "They're going to leave most of the structure standing, as a monument. There'll be a display with pictures of the building, the naturalists will give guided walks explaining how this was the birthplace of the national parks . . . it should generate a lot of interest . . . ."

Jim put his hand on my shoulder and pushed himself up. "Generate a lot of hot air," he said coldly. "Well, some of us in this town got a much better idea."

"What's that?" I asked, getting up with him.

"Gonna light a bomb!" he cried, "under somebody's . . . " A passing motorcycle drowned out his voice, but the intention was clear enough.

"Look in there, kid. Whattaya see?" he demanded. A piece of plywood was missing from the main door. I took a look.

"A bunch of dead leaves in a swimming pool."

"Huh!" he cried, glaring at me.

"Well sure. It's a beautiful old building, Lord knows we're short on them in this country."

"Nah!" He shook his head disgustedly.

"Take it easy, Jim." The old boy looked a little apoplectic.

"Horses, kid. I see horses in the snow. Twenty below. Pulling a 2,000-pound hammer up a pile driver track. Over and over and over again. My old man there, with a whip in his hand, yellin' 'Gid-up!'"

He seemed to be talking to himself. I stood awkwardly, listening.

"Poor dumb animals. Don't know which was dumber, man or beasts. Froze his hands, he did. For a dollar a day, or whatever the hell it was. To put food on the table. Painter was a genius, sure. But he worked with flesh and blood, not just drafting ink. Not just stone and re-bar. You never saw it take shape, kid. Never saw the look on Painter's face when they poured the first arch. Or the look in my Dad's starin' at his bleedin' hands."

He turned and looked at me, poked me in the chest with the pipe stem for emphasis.

"That's the advantage I have on you. You ain't gonna get away with it."

"Get away with what? No one's trying to get . . . "

"No sir!" He patted me kindly on the shoulder.

I got in the truck and waved goodbye.

"Buy yourself a new swimmin' suit, kid," he called after me. "You'll need it, mark my words."

I watched him walk slowly away, leaning heavily on his cane, shoulders hunched, this old man, struck by his conviction that the force of time and neglect could be reversed. And I remembered another summer day long ago, when I'd come to the Cave as a small boy. We'd left the hot, dusty prairie behind and driven into the long blue shadows of high mountains, where you could sleep at night in the cool, pine-scented air. I remembered floating on my back that evening in one of the shallow pools, where the pines seemed to lean together overhead. A grey jay flew over, and a black shadow on the hillside turned into a black bear that faded into a shadow again and was gone, leaving me staring.

I recall the tender way my parents talked to each other, freed for a few moments from worry, pain and anxiety. "I wonder what the poor folks are doing," said my father with a smile. I was mystified: we were the poor folks. He was a trucker who loaded his dump truck with a scoop shovel because he couldn't make enough to hire a loader. He had a bad back, naturally, and was sure the mineral water would make it better.

Warm water bubbled out of the rocks; I stared and stared, wide-eyed. It was a giant's bathtub, or a moat around this castle made of moss and stone. My parents were so happy that I had to squeeze between them and ask, "What is this place?"

"It's the park."

"The park." A place evergreen and full of mischievous, grey-coloured birds quarreling with each other and scolded by the squirrels. Bears were real here, though maybe only children could see them. Mother frowned when you mentioned them. They were magical, like the smell of new canvas, the tent billowing softly that night among the pines. Laughter floated on the breeze. Peering outside through a chink in the nest of sleeping bags, you saw only the red eye of the fire, and a giant shape rising into the stars. Was that a mountain watching you? The red eye blinked out. You were small and safe, tucked away in the big night of the park, and you knew that like any storied land, it would never change.

But nothing in nature remains immutable. Though the world has been transformed almost beyond recognition by man's innovative mind, nature invented change, not man. Mutability burns in every cell that sparkles with its mystery and dies, becomes the sloughed-off matter that breeds new life in its ashes.

These mountains, with their hearts of stone, are no less subject to time's transforming tides. Wind, water, and ice are working everywhere to level them under gravity's invisible hand. But once you leave the highway, the process slows down. Behind the evergreen curtain, you become a time traveller moving into the past. Stare at the compacted earth under your boots. There are the tracks of ancient inhabitants, coyotes, deer, and rarely, the naked five-toed track of a bear. Sometimes you forget that you are not the first human to come this way; the naked foot of man stepped here thousands of years before you.

It's hard to imagine that when, in some remote valley, your voice alone echoes in the distances. Your voice stirs the listeners with their old fear of man. Then you are not dwarfed, as you are on the highways, when all human scale is compared to the infinite. Not that we are not powerful: far from it. We are too powerful, strong enough to suffocate the planet with carbon dioxide, or turn it into a parched desert with hydrogen bombs. Yes, our minds are far too busy with mutability, planning for a future our children may never see unless we learn to slow life down. To take these journeys backward in time is to search for a new future, still connected to the great chain of life, life unbroken.

You have been wandering these trails and climbing these passes for several days now. At first there was a constant ringing in your ears: the sound of civilization. Now it begins to fade. Now you can hear the sound of thoughts opening their petals in your head. You can hear the sound of a pine cone falling a hundred metres away. The further you go into the backcountry, the more you begin to move like a hunter. Now it is a camera, a notebook, the mind's open eye you hunt with, not a spear, a bow, or a rifle.

And then it's time to return. Whatever you found here, it was something you would never find on the corner of Yonge and Bloor. Long before you reach the highway, you can hear the clamour of progress; change, coupled with the profit motive.

Suddenly the noise increases to a deafening roar. Bewildered, a time traveller moving forward again, you step out on the hard surfaces of Banff, Waterton, or Jasper. "How much of this," you ask yourself, looking around with ringing ears, "do we really need?"

Everywhere in the summer parks, you see the faces of the young. For them, history/herstory begins only with their arrival on the scene. God bless them.

In Banff, the old life keeps intruding on the new. The stonecutters building St. Mary's Catholic Church worked with steel hammers to shape its rock walls. But

Kootenay National Park. "The mountains shall bring peace to the people."

whose hand once wielded the grooved maul, made of stone, that was found when the foundation was dug? What people are those whose crumbling bones Warden Gilmar found in a log-burial chamber far up the Red Deer River, north of town? Who built the pit houses that lie, still unexplored, under a fairway on the Banff Springs golf course?

"Probably some crazy Shuswap," answered archaeologist Barney Reeves, when I asked about them. "They tried their plateau salmon-based culture in the Rockies for a little while, gave it up, and left."

No salmon in these ranges; no Shuswap need apply.

These artifacts are another door into the past. They allow conversations across the barriers of time. Perhaps that's why so many urbanites surround themselves with antique furniture, or restore old stone farmhouses at great labour and expense. A person, a nation, does not live only in the present tense. Time and again we have learned, to our chagrin, that we ignore the lessons of the past only to imperil the future.

J. B. Harkin, the first Commissioner of Dominion Parks, was one man who strove to do something concrete to keep the past alive in the national consciousness. He felt that conservation of historic sites and structures, and the commemoration of historic events significant to the whole nation, could be best carried out by the National Parks Branch.

Under his direction, the nation's first historic parks were established at Fort Howe, New Brunswick, in 1914, and Fort Anne, Nova Scotia, in 1917. The National Parks Act of 1930 provided for more historic parks to be established and managed by the National Parks Branch. Today, Parks Canada controls seventy historic parks from coast to coast. In addition, six hundred persons and events important in the nation's history and cultural development have been commemorated by plaques and cairns.

Parks Canada, advised by the Historic Sites and Monuments Board, is working to represent all significant phases of our history and culture, just as it strives to establish national parks that represent all the different life zones of the country. Today archaeologists, museum curators, and artifact conservators are key members of Parks Canada's field staff. Sometimes their work calls for reconstruction of old structures. Such was the case at Fort Anne. Plans originally drawn up by Samuel de Champlain in the 1600s were used to reconstruct the *Habitation*, home of the first French settlers in Canada.

Below the Parliamentary Library in distant Ottawa, the locks of the Rideau Canal, one of the many historic canals administered by Parks Canada, are receiving major renovations.

While a park interpreter looks on, a young girl labours with a mallet and chisel to chip one tiny flake from a granite building block.

"They must have been giants in the olden days," she says, awed by the hardness and size of the stone. Then and there a history lesson begins, at the very point where history was made. Ultimately, history's monuments can only be founded in the human heart.

As you follow the historic parks across the nation more and more of the national story comes alive. At Rocky Mountain House National Historic Park, accessible from the David Thompson Highway in neighbouring Banff Park, the fur trade sets the theme for park interpretation. This was the jumping-off place for David Thompson's exploration of the mountain barrier. Now park archaeologists have unearthed the ruins of old fur forts, and historians have pieced together the story of the fur brigades. The interpreter here is a gruffed-voiced fur trader who takes you on a tour around the site: his voice is contained on a solar-powered cassette tape. He tells you of young Thompson's travels among the fierce Blackfoot Indians, once the terror of the plains. The old muskets and trade goods in the visitor centre here take you on a journey to the days "When Fur was King."

In nearby Banff Park, the interpretive service has become more and more involved in relating the human history of the park. It's obvious that the present development of the Bow Valley, so alien to the modern concept of what national parks should be, cannot be understood without exploring the past.

One of the most important human activities here, in the early years of the park, was coal mining. Substantial ruins of a mining town remain at Bankhead, just north of Banff, which became a ghost town after 1922, when the mine was closed. A self-guiding walkway now takes you on a tour of the ghost town's past. The purpose of the old rusting equipment is explained in pictures and text. In one of the old buildings, a scale model showing the miners working on the sloping coal strata deep inside Cascade Mountain, presents a testament to the skill and courage of the coal miner. The town is a ghostly presence, first welcomed and then shunned as an unsightly addition in the park. Now, on the slag heaps, rhubarb planted long ago by a miner's wife has spread defiantly beyond the bounds of her vanished garden.

Parks Canada, committed to preserving the nation's historic places, had not forgotten about the Cave and Basin's place in the nation's history, either. Although it seemed unlikely that funds could be found to restore the swimming facilities there, proposals were made to stabilize the buildings, and replace the main pool with a commemorative garden. That proposal resulted in a massive public protest, led by two long-time park residents, Vera McGinn and Mary Allan. They founded the "Save the Cave and Basin Swimming Pools Committee," and 21,000 people from all over Canada signed a petition requesting Parks Canada to renovate and restore the entire structure, including the pool.

The wishes of the public, and support from politicians in Ottawa, made it possible for the government to allocate enough funds to make an almost complete redevelopment of Painter's masterpiece. My friend Jim's prediction had come true, though he didn't live long enough to take a plunge in the rebuilt swimming pool.

George Stewart's rustic bathhouses are rebuilt and the Basin, reduced over the years to an unsightly cement tank, has been returned to a more natural state. The Cave and Basin area will look much as it did after Painter's building was finished in 1914.

It's winter at the Cave and Basin Centennial Centre, and Painter's red-roofed belvederes are capped with snow. The freshly-mortared rockwork on the north wall and the new glass gleaming in the massive wind screens make the place look newly-risen from the wooden scaffolding that litters the site.

Masons, painters, electricians and plumbers swarm over the old structure. They work under the protection of a temporary plastic roof. The upper storey of the bathhouse, formerly used only for a storeroom, will house commemorative displays celebrating the birth of the first "nation's park." Wooden walkways take visitors up the terraces to the Cave vent and further to where mineral water bubbles up in steaming pools. Clouds of this steam jet into the frigid air, and thick hoar frost sparkles on the pines and poplar trees.

The walkway leads me down through the spruce trees over the steaming rivulets of warm water. It's a self-guided trail that tells me, through signs and illustrations, about the discovery of the place by McCabe and the McCardells, long ago. And there's the whimsical story of the Banff long-nosed dace, a rare little minnow, being eaten out of house and home by tropical fish that some misguided souls released in this swamp a few years back. That old devil change is busy wreaking subsurface havoc even in this semi-frozen bayou.

Out among the reeds, the boardwalk leads me to a hideaway, a blind made of cedar board where I play peek-a-boo with some confused mallards who are supposed to be in Florida. The open stretch of water here, surrounded by ice on three sides, is kept thawed by the warm runoff from the springs, and that keeps the ducks in winter residence.

And like a good omen at the end of a long trail, I greet an old friend, the water ouzel. I last saw him swimming one winter day in an open lead on the Cascade River, north of Banff. Now here he is again, this slate-gray dipper, smaller than a robin, bobbing up and down on the snowy edge of his private heated pool. Seal-like, he splashes in and, fish-like once in the water, he whisks over the bottom, scooping up some tiny insects. He pops up on the snow again and bobs madly up and down on his toothpick legs, pleased with his own ingenuous nature. And just like I do every time I see this merry bird, defying King Winter, I laugh aloud, as delighted with him as he is with himself.

The laughter echoes over the marsh and startles the ducks into brief flight. They refuse to get used to the sound of a human voice. But human voices, the voices of ancient hunters, the voices of traders, of prospectors, and of modern tourists, have echoed over this swamp for a long time. There is much they wouldn't recognize, those old and savage mountaineers, those genteel visitors and fortune hunters. But there is much that is the same in these ranges, or close enough to the same, to satisfy our growing craving for solitude, for peace. For a future we can inhabit like a familiar room, for a world that is still evergreen and new, where there is time to think, time to feel, time to be entertained by a single bird in a pool of dark water, surrounded by snow.

Dip, little bird. Bob and sing.

Long may you reign, at this birthplace of a grand and fabulous notion.

"An almost complete redevelopment of Painter's masterpiece."

Lifeguards, ca.1930.

Acknowledgements

I am grateful to E. J. Hart and his staff at the Archives of the Canadian Rockies in Banff for showing patience beyond the bounds of good humour to speed my research.

Prof. B. Reeves of the University of Calgary, and Messrs. Don Steer and John Porter of Parks Canada set my feet firmly in the path of archaeological knowledge, but cannot be held responsible for any wrong turns I've made here. Prof. Reeves directed me to the Claude E. Schaeffer Papers, where I found the skin and bones of fact to help flesh out my fanciful creations in Chapter One.

I have a long-standing debt of gratitude to Fergus Lothian of Parks Canada, who keeps as much parks history stored in his head as he does in the commodious and overflowing file cabinets of his Ottawa office.

Ms. L. Taylor of Parks Canada kindly lent me her unpublished history of the Cave and Basin hot springs. Taylor's work, along with Eleanor Luxton's history of Banff, and Janet Foster's account of wildlife preservation in Canada (see bibliography), helped greatly to focus my own research. Another most useful, though ponderous implement, was R. C. Scace's three-volume bibliography of national parks: Mr. Scace put his sole remaining copy at my disposal.

Thanks to Mr. Bob Sandford, Mr. Bruno Engler (photographers), and to Wardens Clair Israelson and Tim Auger for allowing me access to their coloured slide inventories. Jim Deegan, author and raconteur of Banff, reminisced for the record about a few famous oldtimers. William M. Pearce of Toronto shared his memories of his famous father, William Pearce.

A benedicite to my wife Myrna, who finally emerged victorious after a long hard duel with our recalcitrant Smith-Corona.

To all of you, and to anyone I may have missed; happy trails!

Permissions

Every effort has been made by the publisher to obtain permission for the following:

From *The Origin and Meaning of the National Parks of Canada.*

"Extracts from the papers of the late Jas. B. Harkin, first Commissioner of the National Parks of Canada." Compiled by M. B. Williams. Dist. by National Parks Branch, Dept. North. Affairs and National Resources, Saskatoon. "Copyright 1957, by H.R. Larson Publishing Co. All rights reserved."

"Use without abuse — how can it be attained? . . . . them from the outside world." (p. 98)
"People sometimes accuse me . . . . purify the spirit." (p. 95)
"The further we have been from nature . . . . even primitive life." (p. 95)
"Such a life allows man . . . . pleasure in renewing." (p. 97)
"The day will come . . . . primaeval nature retained." (p. 97)

"How could the hardheaded members . . . . to increase parks appropriations?" (p. 98)

From *Nor'West Farmer* Magazine, Winnipeg, 1920.
Article: "The Story of the Cave and its keeper at Banff as told to a member of the Staff." (author unknown)
"Sanderson's Mountain Dew . . . . on with the dance!" (p. 93-4)

From *The Great Railway, 1881-1885,* by Pierre Berton. Used by permission of the Canadian Publishers McClelland and Stewart Ltd., 1971.

"For some of us are bums . . . . on the C.P.R." (p. 31)

Public Archives of Canada

1. *The Macdonald Papers,* vol. 229.
   Letter, Peter Mitchell to John A. Macdonald, July 23, 1885.
   Mitchell reported on the value of the site as being worth "at least half a million of dollars." (p. 37)

2. *The Macdonald Papers,* vol 229.
   Thomas White to John A. Macdonald, Nov. 21, 1885.
   "It would be a great misfortune to permit the springs to get into the hands of any of these claimants." (p. 41)

3. Public Archives of Canada, Ottawa
   RG 84, vol. 535, File 87154
   Letter, W. L. Stewart to the Minister of the Interior, August 29, 1885.
   "before a lease is granted . . . . and other improvements." (p. 40)
   "set aside . . . .as a national park." (p. 41)

4. Dafoe, John W. *Clifford Sifton in Relation to his Times.* Toronto: 1931.
   "It was a department . . . . transacted with it." (p. 74)

Early years at the Cave and Basin.

I passed the tobacco pouch to Jim, feeling like a leper in my park uniform, as he filled his pipe in morose silence. Every time I walked down Banff Avenue, little kids would come up and ask me, ''How come you closed down the swimming pool?'' as if it were my personal decision. Just about everybody in Banff had learned to swim at the old pool.

There had been a lot of good reasons for the decision, of course. Ever since 1916, subsidence, due to the unstable rock, had caused cracks in the pool and part of the structure. Health regulations required chlorination of the water in 1960: pink-eye had become a problem in the warm pool. But chlorination made for an un-sightly and unsafe white sediment in the water which resulted in the closing of the warm pools, and the use of non-mineral water in the big pool.

Visitation declined steadily over the years. The climate in the mountains works against cold-water swimming except on the very hottest days. Without the warm pools, there was no more ''shoulder season'' to keep the revenue up on pool use. It became clear that nothing short of major renovations could stop the rain of ceiling plaster and the cracks in the structure. The place was a public hazard, and renova-tion would be very costly. Painter's old masterpiece had done well by the national park. Now she was out to pasture behind her plywood blinkers until the powers that be decided just what to do with her.

Ancestral Voices

One summer day in 1978, I left the warden office and drove up towards Sundance Canyon on patrol. At the Cave and Basin, an oldtimer I knew (I'll call him Jim) flagged me down, and I pulled over to shoot the breeze with him.

Time had not been kind to Painter's masterpiece. The Cave was no longer the main park attraction to the more sophisticated visitors of our era. The pool was closed, its glass windshields covered with plywood. Those who wished to soak in sulphur water would now have to go to the Upper Hot Springs. It was eerily silent, except for a couple of ravens yacking away. Their voices echoed from the bottom of the empty swimming pool. Vandals had been at work, and bits of broken glass crunched underfoot as I walked over to where the old man sat on the steps of the belvederes.

"Jim, how you been keepin'?"

"Pretty good 'till I come up and seen this mess. What the hell's goin' on? See you got the sun on your face," he added before I could answer. "Ain't been a half-ton jockey all summer, maybe?"

I sat down beside him and began to fill my pipe. "Just came out of the Dormer River," I told him. "Ten-day patrol. Wish I was still there."

His face lit up. He was probably remembering a few bighorns he had poached out there before I was born. "That big shale slope at the summit . . . ."

"Yes?"

"Any goat there?"

"Ten or twelve, every time I ride through there."

"That's something, ain't it?" he said with a smile. "Like you could reach across from the saddle and pull an old billy's beard as you go by . . . ."

"Except for the canyon right under your left foot."

"Glad to hear they're still there," he said softly.

"No thanks to you."

"Ha!" He slapped his leg and grinned. "You know I got too stove up to ride . . . know how old I am? Eighty. But I can still swim." He was silent for a few seconds.

"I come up here to swim, only pool in town you can swim in. And you shut her down."

"Jim, I didn't . . . ."

"Shut her down," he muttered angrily.

To keep pace with developments in mountaineering, the wardens began to train for longer periods of time, using more sophisticated equipment. They practised with the first cable rescue gear developed in Switzerland and, in 1966, used it to lift two stranded climbers from a ledge eighty metres below the summit of Mount Babel (3,101 m.).

Walter Perren succeeded in transforming the park wardens into a capable band of mountaineers. His untimely death in 1967 from leukemia robbed the warden service of their greatest guide, and robbed the mountaineering public of a truly benevolent spirit who was happiest with lots of altitude under his feet. By 1975, when the Banff warden service carried out a record 134 rescues in one year, mountaineering was all in a day's work.

In the last decade, proficiency in mountain rescue has led to Parks Canada's inclusion as the only North American member of ICAR, the International Commission of Alpine Rescue. Much of the credit must go to Walter Perren's successors, Peter Fuhrmann of Banff Park, and Willi Pfisterer of Jasper, regional alpine specialists.

Fuhrmann and Pfisterer have worked aggressively over the years to maintain and improve on international standards for rescue introduced by Perren. Fuhrmann introduced the helicopter sling rescue technique to the parks. This involves slinging one or two wardens in a special harness beneath a helicopter to reach accident sites where the machine cannot land due to the steep terrain.

With the recruiting of wardens from younger generations, the attitude of the service to mountaineering has changed dramatically. A number of wardens have qualified for membership in the Association of Canadian Mountain Guides. Climbing, like skiing, whether downhill, cross-country, or with alpine touring skis, is an established part of the job, all part of life in the Big Time.

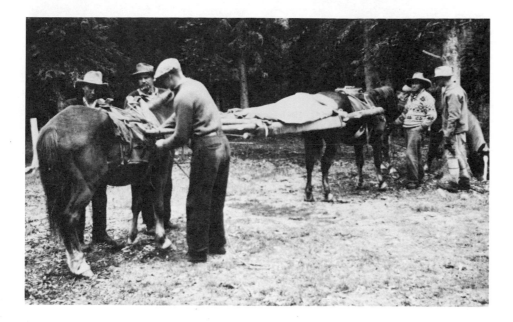

Rescue on horse-slung stretcher.

and down the cliffs like a mountain goat as they clung and clawed at the crumbling holds, learning the ropes.

In those days, nine out of ten wardens were devoted to nicotine. "Walter," some poor smoker would wheeze, with a butt dangling from his lower lip, "how much further is it?" Then high above, where the nylon rope led to some tiny belay stance, the guide's head would poke out into space, smiling down at them.

"It's chust a liddle bit up," he would call encouragingly.

"Chust a liddle bit up," they would mutter angrily; the answer was always the same, whether it was a 200-metre practice cliff, or an "11,000-footer," studded with ice. "Chust a liddle bit up" became their humorous and painful rallying cry.

One of Walter's favourite finishing schools for climbers was Mount Victoria. There is a famous sickle of snow on the south ridge with nothing above it but clouds, and nothing below it but British Columbia on the one hand, and Alberta on the other. Walter used to stroll across this spidery catwalk with the rope playing out behind him, find a good belay spot, and cry out, "Ho-kay, boys." The novice climbers would often take to straddling the nasty thing, inching across on their frozen buns.

"Stand up, boys," said Walter cheerfully. "You won't bump your heads." And the cowboy climbers suddenly realized they had just climbed their first high mountain. It made them smile, despite themselves; some of them actually enjoyed it but they managed to keep that to themselves.

"They give the old place a real facelift back in the late fifties," Jim allowed, "but they should have done some major rebuilding then."

I nodded. "There's just no money for that kind of reconstruction right now. You know, it's kind of questionable if a swimming pool is really appropriate in a national park," I added, lamely.

Jim snorted smoke and yanked the pipe out of his mouth. "Tell it to the ski lifts!" he said sharply.

I sucked unhappily on my own incinerator, silenced by the usual Banff conundrum: on the one hand, grizzly bears; on the other hand, disco city.

"So what are ya gonna do, just let the whole damn place sink into the muck?" demanded Jim.

"Well, it's not up to . . . ," I began, and sighed. The pipe wouldn't stay lit; I put it away. "They're going to leave most of the structure standing, as a monument. There'll be a display with pictures of the building, the naturalists will give guided walks explaining how this was the birthplace of the national parks . . . it should generate a lot of interest . . . . "

Jim put his hand on my shoulder and pushed himself up. "Generate a lot of hot air," he said coldly. "Well, some of us in this town got a much better idea."

"What's that?" I asked, getting up with him.

"Gonna light a bomb!" he cried, "under somebody's . . . " A passing motorcycle drowned out his voice, but the intention was clear enough.

"Look in there, kid. Whattaya see?" he demanded. A piece of plywood was missing from the main door. I took a look.

"A bunch of dead leaves in a swimming pool."

"Huh!" he cried, glaring at me.

"Well sure. It's a beautiful old building, Lord knows we're short on them in this country."

"Nah!" He shook his head disgustedly.

"Take it easy, Jim." The old boy looked a little apoplectic.

"Horses, kid. I see horses in the snow. Twenty below. Pulling a 2,000-pound hammer up a pile driver track. Over and over and over again. My old man there, with a whip in his hand, yellin' 'Gid-up!'"

He seemed to be talking to himself. I stood awkwardly, listening.

"Poor dumb animals. Don't know which was dumber, man or beasts. Froze his hands, he did. For a dollar a day, or whatever the hell it was. To put food on the table. Painter was a genius, sure. But he worked with flesh and blood, not just drafting ink. Not just stone and re-bar. You never saw it take shape, kid. Never saw the look on Painter's face when they poured the first arch. Or the look in my Dad's starin' at his bleedin' hands."

He turned and looked at me, poked me in the chest with the pipe stem for emphasis.

"That's the advantage I have on you. You ain't gonna get away with it."

"Get away with what? No one's trying to get ... "

"No sir!" He patted me kindly on the shoulder.

I got in the truck and waved goodbye.

"Buy yourself a new swimmin' suit, kid," he called after me. "You'll need it, mark my words."

I watched him walk slowly away, leaning heavily on his cane, shoulders hunched, this old man, struck by his conviction that the force of time and neglect could be reversed. And I remembered another summer day long ago, when I'd come to the Cave as a small boy. We'd left the hot, dusty prairie behind and driven into the long blue shadows of high mountains, where you could sleep at night in the cool, pine-scented air. I remembered floating on my back that evening in one of the shallow pools, where the pines seemed to lean together overhead. A grey jay flew over, and a black shadow on the hillside turned into a black bear that faded into a shadow again and was gone, leaving me staring.

I recall the tender way my parents talked to each other, freed for a few moments from worry, pain and anxiety. "I wonder what the poor folks are doing," said my father with a smile. I was mystified: we were the poor folks. He was a trucker who loaded his dump truck with a scoop shovel because he couldn't make enough to hire a loader. He had a bad back, naturally, and was sure the mineral water would make it better.

Warm water bubbled out of the rocks; I stared and stared, wide-eyed. It was a giant's bathtub, or a moat around this castle made of moss and stone. My parents were so happy that I had to squeeze between them and ask, "What is this place?"

"It's the park."

"The park." A place evergreen and full of mischievous, grey-coloured birds quarreling with each other and scolded by the squirrels. Bears were real here, though maybe only children could see them. Mother frowned when you mentioned them. They were magical, like the smell of new canvas, the tent billowing softly that night among the pines. Laughter floated on the breeze. Peering outside through a chink in the nest of sleeping bags, you saw only the red eye of the fire, and a giant shape rising into the stars. Was that a mountain watching you? The red eye blinked out. You were small and safe, tucked away in the big night of the park, and you knew that like any storied land, it would never change.

But nothing in nature remains immutable. Though the world has been transformed almost beyond recognition by man's innovative mind, nature invented change, not man. Mutability burns in every cell that sparkles with its mystery and dies, becomes the sloughed-off matter that breeds new life in its ashes.

These mountains, with their hearts of stone, are no less subject to time's transforming tides. Wind, water, and ice are working everywhere to level them under gravity's invisible hand. But once you leave the highway, the process slows down. Behind the evergreen curtain, you become a time traveller moving into the past. Stare at the compacted earth under your boots. There are the tracks of ancient inhabitants, coyotes, deer, and rarely, the naked five-toed track of a bear. Sometimes you forget that you are not the first human to come this way; the naked foot of man stepped here thousands of years before you.

It's hard to imagine that when, in some remote valley, your voice alone echoes in the distances. Your voice stirs the listeners with their old fear of man. Then you are not dwarfed, as you are on the highways, when all human scale is compared to the infinite. Not that we are not powerful: far from it. We are too powerful, strong enough to suffocate the planet with carbon dioxide, or turn it into a parched desert with hydrogen bombs. Yes, our minds are far too busy with mutability, planning for a future our children may never see unless we learn to slow life down. To take these journeys backward in time is to search for a new future, still connected to the great chain of life, life unbroken.

You have been wandering these trails and climbing these passes for several days now. At first there was a constant ringing in your ears: the sound of civilization. Now it begins to fade. Now you can hear the sound of thoughts opening their petals in your head. You can hear the sound of a pine cone falling a hundred metres away. The further you go into the backcountry, the more you begin to move like a hunter. Now it is a camera, a notebook, the mind's open eye you hunt with, not a spear, a bow, or a rifle.

And then it's time to return. Whatever you found here, it was something you would never find on the corner of Yonge and Bloor. Long before you reach the highway, you can hear the clamour of progress; change, coupled with the profit motive.

Suddenly the noise increases to a deafening roar. Bewildered, a time traveller moving forward again, you step out on the hard surfaces of Banff, Waterton, or Jasper. "How much of this," you ask yourself, looking around with ringing ears, "do we really need?"

Everywhere in the summer parks, you see the faces of the young. For them, history/herstory begins only with their arrival on the scene. God bless them.

In Banff, the old life keeps intruding on the new. The stonecutters building St. Mary's Catholic Church worked with steel hammers to shape its rock walls. But

Kootenay National Park. "The mountains shall bring peace to the people."

whose hand once wielded the grooved maul, made of stone, that was found when the foundation was dug? What people are those whose crumbling bones Warden Gilmar found in a log-burial chamber far up the Red Deer River, north of town? Who built the pit houses that lie, still unexplored, under a fairway on the Banff Springs golf course?

"Probably some crazy Shuswap," answered archaeologist Barney Reeves, when I asked about them. "They tried their plateau salmon-based culture in the Rockies for a little while, gave it up, and left."

No salmon in these ranges; no Shuswap need apply.

These artifacts are another door into the past. They allow conversations across the barriers of time. Perhaps that's why so many urbanites surround themselves with antique furniture, or restore old stone farmhouses at great labour and expense. A person, a nation, does not live only in the present tense. Time and again we have learned, to our chagrin, that we ignore the lessons of the past only to imperil the future.

J. B. Harkin, the first Commissioner of Dominion Parks, was one man who strove to do something concrete to keep the past alive in the national consciousness. He felt that conservation of historic sites and structures, and the commemoration of historic events significant to the whole nation, could be best carried out by the National Parks Branch.

Under his direction, the nation's first historic parks were established at Fort Howe, New Brunswick, in 1914, and Fort Anne, Nova Scotia, in 1917. The National Parks Act of 1930 provided for more historic parks to be established and managed by the National Parks Branch. Today, Parks Canada controls seventy historic parks from coast to coast. In addition, six hundred persons and events important in the nation's history and cultural development have been commemorated by plaques and cairns.

Parks Canada, advised by the Historic Sites and Monuments Board, is working to represent all significant phases of our history and culture, just as it strives to establish national parks that represent all the different life zones of the country. Today archaeologists, museum curators, and artifact conservators are key members of Parks Canada's field staff. Sometimes their work calls for reconstruction of old structures. Such was the case at Fort Anne. Plans originally drawn up by Samuel de Champlain in the 1600s were used to reconstruct the *Habitation*, home of the first French settlers in Canada.

Below the Parliamentary Library in distant Ottawa, the locks of the Rideau Canal, one of the many historic canals administered by Parks Canada, are receiving major renovations.

While a park interpreter looks on, a young girl labours with a mallet and chisel to chip one tiny flake from a granite building block.

"They must have been giants in the olden days," she says, awed by the hardness and size of the stone. Then and there a history lesson begins, at the very point where history was made. Ultimately, history's monuments can only be founded in the human heart.

As you follow the historic parks across the nation more and more of the national story comes alive. At Rocky Mountain House National Historic Park, accessible from the David Thompson Highway in neighbouring Banff Park, the fur trade sets the theme for park interpretation. This was the jumping-off place for David Thompson's exploration of the mountain barrier. Now park archaeologists have unearthed the ruins of old fur forts, and historians have pieced together the story of the fur brigades. The interpreter here is a gruffed-voiced fur trader who takes you on a tour around the site: his voice is contained on a solar-powered cassette tape. He tells you of young Thompson's travels among the fierce Blackfoot Indians, once the terror of the plains. The old muskets and trade goods in the visitor centre here take you on a journey to the days "When Fur was King."

In nearby Banff Park, the interpretive service has become more and more involved in relating the human history of the park. It's obvious that the present development of the Bow Valley, so alien to the modern concept of what national parks should be, cannot be understood without exploring the past.

One of the most important human activities here, in the early years of the park, was coal mining. Substantial ruins of a mining town remain at Bankhead, just north of Banff, which became a ghost town after 1922, when the mine was closed. A self-guiding walkway now takes you on a tour of the ghost town's past. The purpose of the old rusting equipment is explained in pictures and text. In one of the old buildings, a scale model showing the miners working on the sloping coal strata deep inside Cascade Mountain, presents a testament to the skill and courage of the coal miner. The town is a ghostly presence, first welcomed and then shunned as an unsightly addition in the park. Now, on the slag heaps, rhubarb planted long ago by a miner's wife has spread defiantly beyond the bounds of her vanished garden.

Parks Canada, committed to preserving the nation's historic places, had not forgotten about the Cave and Basin's place in the nation's history, either. Although it seemed unlikely that funds could be found to restore the swimming facilities there, proposals were made to stabilize the buildings, and replace the main pool with a commemorative garden. That proposal resulted in a massive public protest, led by two long-time park residents, Vera McGinn and Mary Allan. They founded the "Save the Cave and Basin Swimming Pools Committee," and 21,000 people from all over Canada signed a petition requesting Parks Canada to renovate and restore the entire structure, including the pool.

The wishes of the public, and support from politicians in Ottawa, made it possible for the government to allocate enough funds to make an almost complete redevelopment of Painter's masterpiece. My friend Jim's prediction had come true, though he didn't live long enough to take a plunge in the rebuilt swimming pool.

George Stewart's rustic bathhouses are rebuilt and the Basin, reduced over the years to an unsightly cement tank, has been returned to a more natural state. The Cave and Basin area will look much as it did after Painter's building was finished in 1914.

It's winter at the Cave and Basin Centennial Centre, and Painter's red-roofed belvederes are capped with snow. The freshly-mortared rockwork on the north wall and the new glass gleaming in the massive wind screens make the place look newly-risen from the wooden scaffolding that litters the site.

Masons, painters, electricians and plumbers swarm over the old structure. They work under the protection of a temporary plastic roof. The upper storey of the bathhouse, formerly used only for a storeroom, will house commemorative displays celebrating the birth of the first "nation's park." Wooden walkways take visitors up the terraces to the Cave vent and further to where mineral water bubbles up in steaming pools. Clouds of this steam jet into the frigid air, and thick hoar frost sparkles on the pines and poplar trees.

The walkway leads me down through the spruce trees over the steaming rivulets of warm water. It's a self-guided trail that tells me, through signs and illustrations, about the discovery of the place by McCabe and the McCardells, long ago. And there's the whimsical story of the Banff long-nosed dace, a rare little minnow, being eaten out of house and home by tropical fish that some misguided souls released in this swamp a few years back. That old devil change is busy wreaking sub-surface havoc even in this semi-frozen bayou.

Out among the reeds, the boardwalk leads me to a hideaway, a blind made of cedar board where I play peek-a-boo with some confused mallards who are supposed to be in Florida. The open stretch of water here, surrounded by ice on three sides, is kept thawed by the warm runoff from the springs, and that keeps the ducks in winter residence.

And like a good omen at the end of a long trail, I greet an old friend, the water ouzel. I last saw him swimming one winter day in an open lead on the Cascade River, north of Banff. Now here he is again, this slate-gray dipper, smaller than a robin, bobbing up and down on the snowy edge of his private heated pool. Seal-like, he splashes in and, fish-like once in the water, he whisks over the bottom, scooping up some tiny insects. He pops up on the snow again and bobs madly up and down on his toothpick legs, pleased with his own ingenuous nature. And just like I do every time I see this merry bird, defying King Winter, I laugh aloud, as delighted with him as he is with himself.

The laughter echoes over the marsh and startles the ducks into brief flight. They refuse to get used to the sound of a human voice. But human voices, the voices of ancient hunters, the voices of traders, of prospectors, and of modern tourists, have echoed over this swamp for a long time. There is much they wouldn't recognize, those old and savage mountaineers, those genteel visitors and fortune hunters. But there is much that is the same in these ranges, or close enough to the same, to satisfy our growing craving for solitude, for peace. For a future we can inhabit like a familiar room, for a world that is still evergreen and new, where there is time to think, time to feel, time to be entertained by a single bird in a pool of dark water, surrounded by snow.

Dip, little bird. Bob and sing.

Long may you reign, at this birthplace of a grand and fabulous notion.

"An almost complete redevelopment of Painter's masterpiece."

Lifeguards, ca.1930.

Acknowledgements

I am grateful to E. J. Hart and his staff at the Archives of the Canadian Rockies in Banff for showing patience beyond the bounds of good humour to speed my research.

Prof. B. Reeves of the University of Calgary, and Messrs. Don Steer and John Porter of Parks Canada set my feet firmly in the path of archaeological knowledge, but cannot be held responsible for any wrong turns I've made here. Prof. Reeves directed me to the Claude E. Schaeffer Papers, where I found the skin and bones of fact to help flesh out my fanciful creations in Chapter One.

I have a long-standing debt of gratitude to Fergus Lothian of Parks Canada, who keeps as much parks history stored in his head as he does in the commodious and overflowing file cabinets of his Ottawa office.

Ms. L. Taylor of Parks Canada kindly lent me her unpublished history of the Cave and Basin hot springs. Taylor's work, along with Eleanor Luxton's history of Banff, and Janet Foster's account of wildlife preservation in Canada (see bibliography), helped greatly to focus my own research. Another most useful, though ponderous implement, was R. C. Scace's three-volume bibliography of national parks: Mr. Scace put his sole remaining copy at my disposal.

Thanks to Mr. Bob Sandford, Mr. Bruno Engler (photographers), and to Wardens Clair Israelson and Tim Auger for allowing me access to their coloured slide inventories. Jim Deegan, author and raconteur of Banff, reminisced for the record about a few famous oldtimers. William M. Pearce of Toronto shared his memories of his famous father, William Pearce.

A benedicite to my wife Myrna, who finally emerged victorious after a long hard duel with our recalcitrant Smith-Corona.

To all of you, and to anyone I may have missed; happy trails!

Permissions

Index

Bibliography

Anderson, Frank W. *Calgary Banff Highway.* Calgary: Frontier Publishing, 1968.

Berton, Pierre. *The National Dream, The Great Railway, 1871-1881.* Toronto: McClelland and Stewart Ltd., 1970.

—*The Last Spike, The Great Railway, 1881-1885.* Toronto: McClelland and Stewart Ltd., 1971.

Carter, David J. *Behind Canadian Barbed Wire.* Calgary: Tumbleweed Press Ltd., 1980.

Creighton, Donald. *Dominion of the North, A History of Canada.* Toronto: The Macmillan Company of Canada, Ltd., 1966.

Fleming, Sir Sandford. *England and Canada, A Summer Tour Between Old and New Westminister.* London: Sampson, Low, et al., 1884.

Foster, Janet. *Working for Wildlife, the Beginnings of Preservation in Canada.* Toronto: University of Toronto Press, 1978.

Hart, E. J. *The Diamond Hitch, The Early Outfitters of Banff and Jasper.* Banff: Summerthought, 1979.

—*The Selling of Canada.* Banff: Altitude Publishing Ltd., 1983.

Lothian, W. F. *A History of Canada's National Parks,* volumes 1-1V. Ottawa: Parks Canada, 1976-1981.

Luxton, Eleanor G. *Banff, Canada's First National Park, A History and a Memory of Rocky Mountains Park.* Banff: Summerthought, 1975.

MacGregor, James G. *A History of Alberta.* Edmonton: Hurtig Publishers Ltd., 1981.

Nelson, J. G., ed. *Canadian Parks in Perspective.* Montreal: Harvest House Ltd., 1970.

Nelson, J. G. and Scace, R. C., eds. *The Canadian National Parks Today and Tomorrow.* Studies in land use history and landscape change, National Park Series No. 3. Calgary: Duplicating Services, The University of Calgary, 1968.

Robinson, Bart. *Banff Springs, The Story of a Hotel.* Banff: Summerthought, 1973.

Scace, R. C. *Banff, Jasper, Kootenay and Yoho,* *An Initial Bibliography of the Contiguous Canadian Rocky Mountains National Parks.* Ottawa: National and HIstoric Parks Branch, 1973.

Southesk, James Carnegie, Earl. *Saskatchewan and the Rocky Mountains.* Reprint. Edmonon: M. G. Hurtig Ltd., 1969.

Spry, Irene M. *The Palliser Expedition.* Toronto: The Macmillan Co. of Canada Ltd., 1963.

Strom, Erling. *Pioneers on Skis.* Central Valley, N.Y.: Smith Clove Press, 1977.

Sutton, Ann and Sutton, Myron. *Yellowstone, A Century of the Wilderness Idea.* New York: The Macmillan Co., 1972.

Williams, Mabel B. *The History and Meaning of the National Parks in Canada.* Saskatoon: H. R. Lawson Publishing, 1957.

Wilson, Thomas E. *Trail Blazer of the Canadian Rockies.* ed. Hugh A. Dempsey. Calgary: Glenblow Alberta Institute, 1972.

Periodicals, Government Reports, Articles

Department of the Interior (Canada). "Annual Reports." Ottawa: Pub. by Gov. of Canada, 1887-1932.

Government of Canada. "Commons Debates, An Act Respecting the Rocky Mountains Park of Canada, 50-51 Victoria." Ottawa: Pub. by Gov. of Canada, 1887.

International Union for the Conservation of Nature. "Resolutions on National Parks." *Biological Conservation,* vol. 111, No. 2, 1971.

Macdonald, Agnes. "By Car and By Cowcatcher." *Murray's* Magazine, vol. 1, Jan.-June, 1887.

National Parks Branch, Department of Northern Affairs and National Resources. "National Parks Policy." Pamphlet. Ottawa: Pub. by Gov. of Canada, 1964.

National and Historic Parks Branch. "Banff National Park Provisional Master Plan." Ottawa: Queen's Printer for Canada, 1969.

Nor'West Farmer Magazine. "The Story of the Cave and its Keeper at Banff, Alberta." Autumn 1920.

Parks Canada, Indian and Northern Affairs. "Parks Canada Policy." Ottawa: Pub. Programme Policy Group, Parks Canada, 1978.

Unpublished Materials

Banff, Archives of the Canadian Rockies. "The Bill Peyto Collection."

—"Letter of Will Fear." The Norman Luxton Papers.

—"Reminiscenses of a Western Pioncer" by William McCardell.

Banff, Banff National Park Library. "Historic File." Reports and Official Correspondence, Park Development and Human History.

Ottawa, Public Archives of Canada. The Macdonald Papers, vol. 229. "Peter Mitchell to John A. Macdonald. July 23, 1885." "Thomas White to John A. Macdonald. November 21, 1885."

Ottawa, Public Archives of Canada. Record Groups 15 and 84, numerous records relating to the history of the Canadian National Parks. See particularly the following: RG 84, vol. 535, file 87154. History of the hot springs at Banff. RG 84, vol. 191, file B 56-20, vol. 2. Building of the Cave and Basin hot springs bathhouse and swimming pool, 1912-1914. RG 84, vol. 51, file BU 209. RG 84, vol. 115. file U 43. The Pablo-Allard buffalo herd. History of the herd and account of its acquisition and disposal by Canadian authorities. RG 84, vol. 232, file 559260. Reservations for park purposes along the CPR right-of-way, 1885-1887.

(For further information on PAC record groups, see Scace, op. cit.)

Pearce, William. "Establishment of National Parks in the Rockies." Ms in collection of William M. Pearce, Toronto.

Schaeffer, Claude E. Ms notes on the ethnography of the Kootenay Indians. Glenbow Alberta Institute, Calgary.

Taylor, L. A. "The Cave and Basin — Birthplace of National Parks." Author's Copy of Ms commissioned by Parks Canada.

Canada's National and National Historic Parks

◯ National Historic Parks

▢ National Parks

—·—· Canada/U.S. Border

National Historic Parks

British Columbia
1 Fort Rodd Hill
2 Fisgard Lighthouse
3 St. Roch
4 Fort Langley
5 Kitwanga
6 Fort St. James
Alberta
7 Rocky Mountain House
Yukon
8 Klondike Sites
9 S.S. Klondike
Saskatchewan
10 Fort Walsh
11 Cypress Hills Massacre
12 Battleford
13 Batoche
14 Fort Espérance
Manitoba
15 Lower Fort Garry
16 Riel House
17 Fort Prince of Wales
18 York Factory

Ontario
19 Fort St. Joseph
20 Fort Malden
21 Woodside
22 Fort George
23 Butler's Barracks
24 Queenston Heights and
   Brock's Monument
25 Kingston Martello Towers
26 Bellevue House
27 Battle of the Windmill
28 Fort Wellington
29 Rideau Canal
30 Bethune Memorial House
Québec
31 Fort Témiscamingue
32 Coteau-du-Lac
33 Sir Wilfrid Laurier House
34 Fort Chambly
35 Fort Lennox
36 Les Forges du Saint-Maurice
37 The Fortifications of Québec
38 Artillery Park
39 Cartier-Brébeuf
40 National Battlefields of
   Québec
41 Fort No. 1
42 Battle of the Châteauguay
43 Louis S. Saint-Laurent
44 Jacques Cartier Monument

New Brunswick
45 Beaubears Island
46 St. Andrews Blockhouse
47 Carleton Martello Tower
48 Survival of the Acadians
49 Fort Beauséjour
Nova Scotia
50 Fort Edward
51 Grand Pré
52 Fort Anne
53 Port Royal
54 Halifax Waterfront Buildings
55 Halifax Citadel
56 Prince of Wales Martello
   Tower
57 York Redoubt
58 Fortress of Louisbourg
59 Alexander Graham Bell
Prince Edward Island
60 Fort Amherst
61 Province House
Newfoundland
62 Port au Choix
63 L'Anse aux Meadows
64 Signal Hill
65 Cape Spear
66 Castle Hill

National Parks

British Columbia
1 Pacific Rim
2 Mount Revelstoke
3 Glacier
4 Yoho
5 Kootenay
Alberta
6 Waterton Lakes
7 Banff
8 Jasper
9 Elk Island
10 Wood Buffalo
Yukon
11 Kluane
Northwest Territories
12 Nahanni
13 Auyuittuq
Saskatchewan
14 Prince Albert
15 Grasslands
Manitoba
16 Riding Mountain

Ontario
17 Pukaskwa
18 Georgian Bay Islands
19 Point Pelée
20 St. Lawrence Islands
Québec
21 La Mauricie
22 Forillon
New Brunswick
23 Kouchibouguac
24 Fundy
Prince Edward Island
25 Prince Edward Island
Nova Scotia
26 Kejimkujik
27 Cape Breton Highlands
Newfoundland
28 Gros Morne
29 Terra Nova